Undiscovered Islands of the Caribbean

Undiscovered Islands of the Caribbean

Fourth Edition

Burl Willes

John Muir Publications
Santa Fe, New Mexico

An RDR Syndicate Production
John Muir Publications, P.O. Box 613, Santa Fe, NM 87504

© 1988, 1990, 1992, 1995 by RDR Syndicate
Cover and maps © 1988, 1990, 1992, 1995 by John Muir Publications
Printed in the United States of America

Fourth edition. First printing September 1995

Library of Congress Cataloging-in-Publication Data
    Willes, Burl, 1941-
    Undiscovered islands of the Caribbean / Burl Willes. — 4th ed.
        p. cm.
    Includes index.
     ISBN 1-56261-239-5 (paperback)
     1. Hotels—Caribbean Area—Guidebooks. 2. Restaurants—Caribbean
Area—Guidebooks. 3. Caribbean Area—Guidebooks. I. Title.
TX907.5.C27W55 1995
647.9472901—dc20   95-16327
                                                               CIP

Production: Kathryn Lloyd-Strongin, Janine Lehmann
Design: Mary Shapiro
Illustrations: Vincent L. Costa
Cover and maps: Holly Wood
Typography: Copygraphics, Santa Fe, New Mexico
Printer: Malloy Lithographing

Distributed to the book trade by
Publishers Group West
Emeryville, California

CONTENTS

CONTENTS

ACKNOWLEDGMENTS

People to whom I am indebted for prior work on earlier editions include Robin and Derk Richardson; Raju Mann Ward, Belize; Lorie and David Brillinger, Islas Mujeres; Dave Fogerty, Isla Holbox; and Eileen Ecklund, Venezuela. In the current edition, I want to convey special thanks to intelligent and intrepid traveler Eileen Ecklund, who wrote the chapter on the Bay Islands of Honduras. She and Randy Zebell returned with much enthusiasm and great photos. Thank you also to Peter Beren, Roger Rapoport, and the staff of John Muir Publications for their help.

INTRODUCTION

The notion of a Caribbean vacation conjures up familiar images of St. Thomas, Jamaica, Puerto Rico, and Trinidad. There are, however, thousands of undiscovered islands in the Caribbean. Most of them are uninhabited. But between the well-known tourist spots—with their time-share condos, crowded beaches, and duty-free shopping—and the deserted barren cays, dozens of secluded islands with friendly populations await the adventurous traveler. Although one can still find beauty and tranquility on the larger and more popular islands, such undiscovered islands as Saba, Marie-Galante, Culebra, and the others described herein offer an escape to a seemingly bygone era, when the Caribbean was unspoiled by high-rise hotels, skyrocketing costs, ungainly crowds, and traffic jams. Many of these islands are rarely visited by more than a few dozen tourists at any one time. Some are so undiscovered that inhabitants of nearby islands may not even know whether or not they are populated.

For this fourth edition, it was a real pleasure to return to the islands and find them, with just one exception, still undiscovered. There are now more choices in accommo-

Quiet mountain road in Montserrat

dations and restaurants, but visitors are still greeted by friendly local residents on islands characterized by a quiet, unhurried lifestyle.

Also encouraging, many islands have taken steps to preserve the land and wildlife from exploitation. In the Turks and Caicos Islands, for example, there are five bird sanctuaries, 13 national parks, and nine nature preserves. Even tiny Carriacou in the Grenadines has proposed a national park.

Off Honduras we found three gems to add to our undiscovered islands list: Utila, Guanaja, and Roatan. Here, as on almost all small islands, the local people are trying to encourage a certain amount of tourism to bolster the local economy and preserve the land.

Encountering the unexpected is what makes traveling to these islands so special. They are full of marvelous surprises, from the natural splendor of the landscape, to the enduring reminders of the regions' fascinating histories, to the intimate details of gracious hospitality.

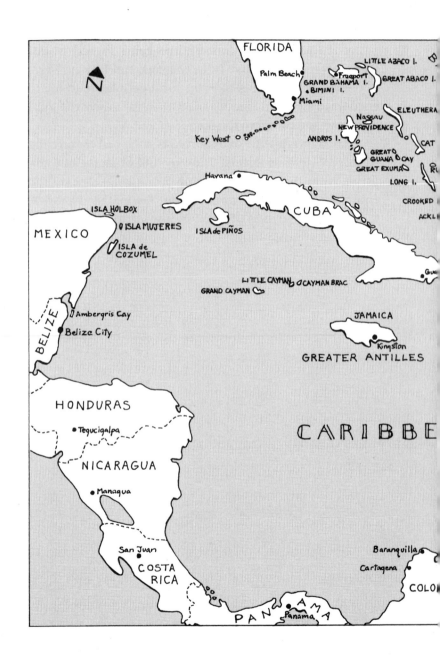

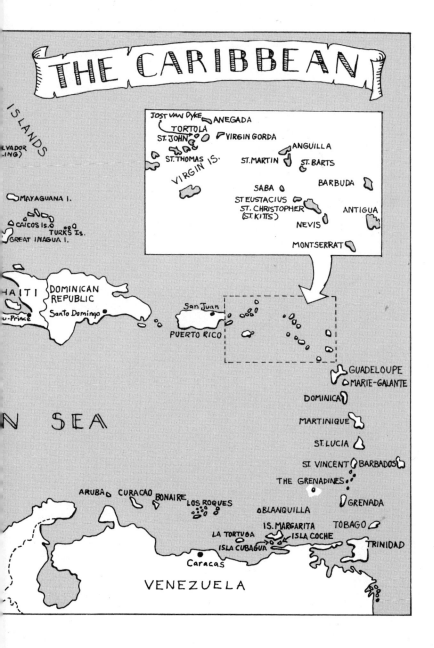

THE CARIBBEAN

ISLANDS

ALVADOR
(ING)

MAYAGUANA I.

CAICOS Is.
TURKS Is.
GREAT INAGUA I.

HAITI
u-Prince

DOMINICAN REPUBLIC
Santo Domingo

JOST VAN DYKE
TORTOLA
ST. JOHN
ST. THOMAS
VIRGIN IS.
ANEGADA
VIRGIN GORDA
ANGUILLA
ST. MARTIN
ST. BARTS
SABA
ST. EUSTACIUS
ST. CHRISTOPHER (ST. KITTS)
NEVIS
BARBUDA
ANTIGUA
MONTSERRAT

San Juan
PUERTO RICO

GUADELOUPE
MARIE-GALANTE
DOMINICA
MARTINIQUE
ST. LUCIA
ST. VINCENT
BARBADOS
THE GRENADINES
GRENADA

N SEA

ARUBA
CURACAO
BONAIRE
LOS ROQUES
O BLANQUILLA
IS. MARGARITA
LA TORTUGA
ISLA COCHE
ISLA CUBAGUA
TOBAGO
TRINIDAD

Caracas

VENEZUELA

THE BAHAMAS

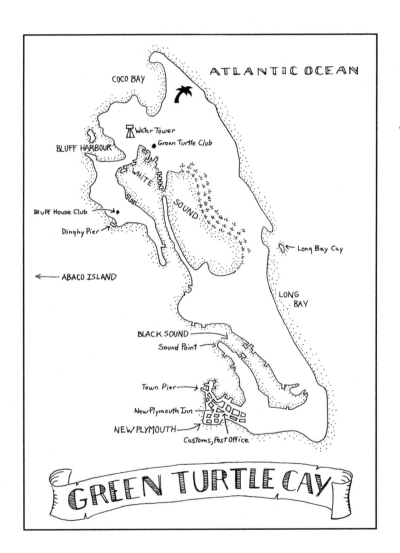

GREEN TURTLE CAY

Green Turtle Cay, The Abacos

The Abacos, located slightly more than 100 miles north of Nassau and 200 miles northeas of Miami, are gradually outgrowing their status as "out" or Family Islands in the Bahamas. Marsh Harbor, on Great Abaco, is a developed commercial center. Walker's Cay and Treasure Cay are luxury resort areas. But Green Turtle Cay, a short ferry ride from Treasure Cay, retains much of the charm of its late-18th-century origins, especially in its main settlement of New Plymouth, a storybook village with narrow streets and old New England-style clapboard buildings painted in bright whites and delicious pastels. New Plymouth provides a delightful trip back in time, while other aspects of Green Turtle Cay are perfect for the vacationer who wants to enjoy the water activities of the Bahamas, without the high life of shopping and gambling.

Like much of the Abacos, Green Turtle Cay was settled in the late 1700s by British Loyalists who exiled themselves from the United States after the revolutionary war. Descendants of the Loyalists and their slaves are the main inhabitants of the island today, where such family names as

Lowe and Sawyer are still predominant. Again in the Abaco tradition, Green Turtle was once known for its fine boat building. Pineapple farming was also a major activity. But today the restful island depends largely on fishing, services, and the small tourist trade.

New Plymouth is situated on a small peninsula with a main harbor at one end and the smaller ferry dock facing in on Black Sound. As we approached the town on the tiny Green Turtle Ferry, we could have been sailing into an old fishing village on the northeastern coast of colonial America. On every little immaculate street, hand-painted signs request Keep GTC Clean, and people comply with such thoroughness that it leaves a modern city dweller dumbfounded. A stroll through this genuinely quaint village takes you along tidy, paved streets that are essentially broad sidewalks, past the whitewashed picket fences that surround private gardens ablaze with colorful flowers. Neatly appointed houses sport gaily painted dormers and gingerbread trim. Children, many of whom look very much alike because of the close family ties, ride by on bicycles. And a few tiny cars and minivans move slowly down the streets. The town includes several stores, a few restaurants, a fascinating museum, and a half-dozen churches representing several different denominations.

Much of the tourist trade is concentrated on White Sound, across the bay from New Plymouth, where the Green Turtle Club and Bluff House welcome the largest number of aquatically inclined guests. From New Plymouth it is a short ride on the Green Turtle Ferry or a long, hot walk around Black Sound. But if you walk, you can take a detour to the ocean side of the island for the best shelling.

(Note: if you walk, be sure to ask for specific directions to wherever you are going. And ask again until you are sure, for Green Turtle's roads branch off in many directions. We walked in circles on the way to Bluff House, ending up at the back of the Green Turtle Club three different times.) Just beyond the two resorts, crescent-shaped Coco Bay sits with calm shallow waters in a palm-lined cove.

Activity peaks on Green Turtle on New Year's Day, when locals celebrate the capture of "Bunce," a folkloric figure who hid in Abaco's forests; in May, during the annual fishing tournament; and during the week of July 4, for the sailing regatta. But for most of the year, the sense of harmony and well-being is undisturbed on this Bahamian Family Island. You step into a way of life that is determined not by the whims and fancies of high-rolling tourists, but by the modest needs and traditional patterns of Green Turtle Cay's peaceful residents.

NOTEWORTHY

Miss Emily's Blue Bee Bar, in New Plymouth on Parliament Street, is famous for the Goombay Smash, a fruity rum drink that Miss Emily blends according to her own secret recipe. The simple two-room bar is the most popular watering hole in New Plymouth, and hundreds of off-islanders have left their business cards tacked to the walls. And the ice-cold Goombay Smash is as delicious and potent as Miss Emily is charming.

The Albert Lowe Museum is housed in a pretty, 150-year-old, green-trimmed white building near the New Plymouth Club and Inn. It is owned by Alton Lowe, a renowned Abaco painter whose work depicting the Abaco people and their way of life is featured on the island's stamps. Exhibits include artwork, shell collections, artifacts from the earliest days of settlement, and ship models built by Alton's father, Albert Lowe.

The Loyalist Memorial Sculpture Garden, across the street from the New Plymouth Club and Inn, was dedicated on November 14, 1987. It features 24 bronze busts of early Loyalists, arranged in the pattern of the Union Jack around a central pedestal with two female figures, one white and one black. The garden is testimony to the degree that this settlement reveres and stays close to its historical roots.

Rooster's Rest Pub and Restaurant, on a low hill on the outskirts of New Plymouth, is the hot spot on weekend nights. The local band, the Gully Roosters, plays Caribbean dance music, mostly soca and reggae, that keeps the spacious bar jumping with a large, integrated crowd of dancers. The energy of both the band and the patrons seems boundless, but anyone needing a breather steps out on the broad deck and rests beneath a black sky studded with millions of shimmering stars.

WHERE TO STAY

New Plymouth Club and Inn
New Plymouth
Green Turtle Cay, Abaco, Bahamas
Telephone: (809) 365-4161; fax: (809) 365-4138
If you have arranged ahead to stay at this charming antique inn, Wally Davies will meet you at the ferry dock and transport you the two or three blocks in his electric golf cart.

A typical house in New Plymouth

The eight rooms in the pink-and-white building are immaculate, with carpets, lace curtains, ceiling fans, and antique furniture. Wally and his wife, Patty, are gracious but not doting hosts. Wally's almost shy demeanor and wry sense of humor make him an unusual and ingratiating innkeeper. He and Patty preside over meals in the tastefully decorated dining area, which has a comfortable indoor room and a canvas-walled porch that extends toward the garden swimming pool. The dinners, featuring some elements of native cuisine, are prepared by Bahamian cooks. Rates are $120 double (plus hotel tax and service), including breakfast and dinner.

Harbour View Apartments
P.O. Box 282
Green Turtle Cay, Abaco, Bahamas
Telephone: (809) 365-4178
These simple beachfront cottages are tucked away in 19 acres of coconut palms, citrus and banana trees, hibiscus, and bougainvillea. Located one-half mile from New Plymouth by footpath, they rent for $85 for a one-bedroom ($550 per week).

Green Turtle Club
Green Turtle Cay, Abaco, Bahamas
Telephone: (809) 365-4271; fax: (809) 365-4272;
U.S. Telephone: (800) 688-4752
The hub of dive and sailing activity on Green Turtle Cay, the sprawling club has 30 rooms scattered around garden-like grounds. The knotty pine dining room and richly decorated bar, festooned with hundreds of sailing flags, are

focal points of social activity among tourists. Lunch—including conch burgers and fritters—is served on an attractive patio overlooking the marina. The club is the island's only four-star resort. Candelight dining by reservation for dinner.

Bluff House
Green Turtle Cay, Abaco, Bahamas
Telephone: (809) 367-4247; fax: (809) 365-4248
Bluff House commands the best hotel vista on Green Turtle Cay. Situated on the cay's highest point, a 100-foot knoll, the main house and dining room look out across the sound for a beautiful view of New Plymouth. Its cottages and condominium-style accommodations are arranged on the slope toward a fine beach. Rates are $90 double, $110 for suites.

RESTAURANTS

At the Sea View, in "downtown" New Plymouth, Betty and Alphonso offer native Bahamian dishes and homemade pies. Dinner reservations required.

Plymouth Rock, near the main dock in New Plymouth, also serves Bahamian specialties and is open for breakfast, lunch, and dinner.

Laura's Snack Bar is a homey little hideaway on a back street behind the New Plymouth Inn. Formerly a cook at the Inn, Laura now prepares home-cooked specialties, including chicken and fish, peas 'n' rice, coleslaw, macaroni salads, several kinds of pie, and homemade ice cream.

Rooster's Rest Pub and Restaurant offers lunches of conch, chicken, burgers, and various sandwiches.

FROM MY JOURNAL

A traveling Pentecostal crusade has set up its striped tent on the vacant corner lot across from the New Plymouth Inn. Only two dozen worshipers attend the Saturday night revival. More curious onlookers are standing around in the street. The village's established churches are holding their own services tonight, as well, the sermons and choir music wafting from open windows into the warm night air. Walking down the dimly lit streets, we arrive at Miss Emily's Blue Bee Bar. Here's the action. We order our Goombay Smashes and continue walking under the moonlight. Over the hill at Rooster's Rest, the crowd is feverish. Dancing to the Gully Roosters. We watch, dance, then step outside for air and watch the stars. We walk again, out along the still harbor and through the tranquil back streets of New Plymouth. Homemade ice cream at Laura's. It's wondrous that places like this even exist. The air is like velvet, the night is magical, the sense of peace carries us away.

HOW TO GET THERE

There are direct flights daily from West Palm Beach, Ft. Lauderdale, and Miami via U.S. Air, Island Express, American Eagle, and Paradise Island Air to Treasure Cay airstrip on Abaco Island. Green Turtle Cay is three miles from Abaco. After clearing customs and immigration, hop a cab ($4 per person) for the short trip to the ferry dock. Here you'll board a water taxi ($8 per person) that meets all flights on arrival and departure.

Long Island

After you land at the Deadman's Cay airstrip on Long Island and pick up your luggage, you might find yourself all alone outside the matchbox airport, which is closed and locked up in a matter of minutes after the flight arrives. You quickly begin to sense the real barrenness and desolation connoted by the airfield's name. If you have not already made arrangements for ground transportation, a few taxis will usually be on hand outside. Before he leaves, the airport manager can also make the necessary phone calls for you. Most travelers come to visit the Stella Maris Inn at the northern end of Long Island. But if you land at Deadman's Cay, be prepared for a rugged two-hour ride over a road where the potholes rival the pavement for total space.

Long Island, located 150 miles south of Nassau, was called "Yuma" by the Arawak Indians and "Fernandina" by Columbus after he visited it in 1492. Life could not have been all that much quieter on these 400 square miles five centuries ago. Stretching 90 miles north to south, the island has supported sheep farming, salt extraction operations,

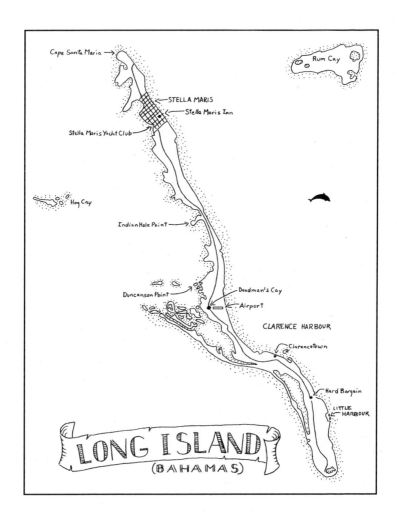

fishing, agriculture (pineapples, bananas, papayas, and corn), and boat building during its history. The largest segment of the population of 3,300 lives near the middle of the island, in and around Deadman's Cay, which is adjoined by such settlements as Lower Deadman's Cay, MacKenzie, Buckley's, Cartwright, and Mangrove Bush. Government Road runs north through Salt Pond, locale of the annual Long Island Regatta; and Simms, an 18th-century seaport; to Stella Maris and Cape Santa Maria. To the south, the road leads to Clarence Town, the island's capital, the Public and Chancery ponds, Hard Bargain, and South End. The adventurous explorer who can withstand miles of bad road will be able to investigate dozens of old Anglican and Catholic churches, such as St. Joseph's near Salt Pond, and St. Paul's and St. Peter's in Clarence Town. There are plantation ruins and attractive beaches in the southernmost reaches.

A quiet beach on the way to Clarence Town

Photo by Derk Richardson

The western shores of Long Island, facing Exuma Sound, have the shallowest and gentlest waters, not unlike many coastlines in the Bahamas. But toward the northeast the terrain is hilly, and the coastline is surprisingly rugged and rocky. The waters here are especially good for scuba diving, with over 20 different spots identified for separate dives. With guidance from the dive masters at Stella Maris, you can even take a controlled dive to swim with the sharks at Shark Reef. Exploring colonial settlements that have changed slowly over time, enjoying the varied water sports and activities at Cape Santa Maria, and just getting away from nearly every sign of civilization are reasons for a visit to this completely different sort of Long Island.

WHERE TO STAY

Stella Maris Inn and Estate
Box 105
Long Island, Bahamas
Telephone: (809) 338-2051; fax: (305) 359-8238;
U.S. Telephone: (800) 426-0466
Dominating the hills at the northern end of Long Island, this luxury resort sprawls out across acres and acres of scenic landscape dotted with coconut palms. Perhaps the effort required to get to Long Island deserves to be rewarded with a stay at this supremely attractive inn. Managed by two solicitous Germans, Peter Kuska and Jorg Friese, Stella Maris can accommodate 140 guests in a variety of rooms, cottages, townhouses, villas, and deluxe bungalows. There are three swimming pools on the vast

grounds and six beaches within walking distance. Scuba diving is a specialty, and waterskiing and boat charters are available. The inn has its own airstrip, tennis courts, dining room, and coffee shop, plus a reciprocal arrangement with the Cape Santa Maria Beach Club nine miles away on the powder-white sand of the Cape Santa Maria lagoon. Rates start at $95 single, $110 double for simple rooms, and go up from there. Modified American Plan is available, as are package arrangements that include airfare and/or scuba diving and fishing. There is no charge for sailing, twice-weekly boat cruises, or bicycles. The hotel provides direct air service from Ft. Lauderdale for $180 one way per person, $90 from Nassau, and $60 from George Town.

J.B. Carroll's Guest House

Deadman's Cay
Long Island, Bahamas
Telephone: (809) 337-1048

For $50 a night, J.B. Carroll will put you up in one of the six bedrooms of his informal guest house, next to his market located on Government Road. He will pick you up at the airport if you call when you land and will rent you one of his cars or jeeps so you can explore the island. In the morning he serves coffee in the dining room of his own house in back. The Carroll guest rooms are homey but very small and simple. They share three bathrooms. Around 11:00 at night J.B. turns off his generator, so out go your lights and off goes the fan.

Photo courtesy of Turks and Caicos Tourist Bureau

Lobster catch at Stella Maris

RESTAURANTS

Conchy's: Carole Archer cried for three months when her husband, Lamond ("Lammy"), told her he was retiring from Xerox and they were moving from Nassau to Long Island. But in less than six months, she decided she loved the remote island life. Now she helps Lammy run this small, homey restaurant just a mile or so south of Stella Maris. Lammy has committed himself to learning his native Bahamian cuisine and has mastered a variety of dishes. Proudly, he showed us his kitchen and let us sample the steamed turtle and the minced lobster. His touch is well worth the $8 to $12 for dinner.

Thompson Bay Inn: At Salt Pond, on the road between Deadman's Cay and Stella Maris, this modest restaurant bar serves excellent local seafood. If you call ahead, dinner will be ready when you arrive. We dropped in on our drive from Deadman's Cay to Stella Maris and returned to find a fresh, hearty meal waiting for us at the appointed time. The grouper and snapper are fried with native spices and served with spicy coleslaw, potato salad, and peas 'n' rice. At about $8, dinner is a rare Bahamian bargain. Breakfasts are around $5, and fish (or conch) and chips snacks run about $4.

HOW TO GET THERE

Bahamasair flies from Nassau and Ft. Lauderdale—sometimes by way of George Town—Exuma, to Deadman's Cay.

The Exumas

During the drive from the tiny airport to the main settlement of George Town, Great Exuma, you begin to realize that having reached the Exumas, only 135 miles southeast of Nassau, you are downshifting into the tranquil pace that continues to slow as you move south in the Bahamas. A taxi driver removes you from the momentary commotion that surrounds arrivals and departures at the airstrip and transports you the few miles to George Town, a one-road town that is a fascinating mix of grand public and rustic private buildings. Although the majority of accommodations are located here, the town has a pervasively sleepy feeling that is extremely conducive to worry-free relaxation and meditative strolls. Except in regatta and fishing contest seasons, this is as quickly as the pulse races in life in the Exumas.

The Exumas are comprised of some 90 miles of cays, with a population of 3,700. Most people live on Great and Little Exuma, with 800 "concentrated" in George Town. The island's colonial history took its most significant turn in the late 1700s, when Denys Rolle took possession of 7,000 acres on Great Exuma and established five cotton plantations worked by his transplanted slaves. Cotton never really succeeded as a cash crop on Exuma, and Rolle's son, Lord John Rolle, presided over a failing empire until his slaves gained emancipation 1834. The Rolle land and name were subsequently passed down through the descendants of his slaves. Today it is still the most prominent family name on Great Exuma. In the 1950s, Jeremiah Rolle introduced tractor farming to the Exumas and cultivated crops of giant sweet potatoes. When you land at the George Town airport,

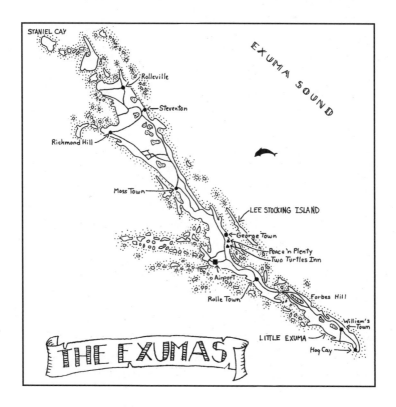

one of the first things you see is the sign reading "Kermit's" marking the bar/restaurant of Kermit Rolle, one of the island's leading entrepreneurs, who also owns the Hilltop Tavern in (where else but?) Rolleville. The architecture of George Town, like most of the settlements in the Exumas, harks back to earlier centuries and proudly displays the islanders' penchant for pastel paints, especially pink and yellow. In the bend where the road curves around the point of beautiful Elizabeth Harbour, an enormous, broad-reaching tree spreads its limbs above a small but lovely Straw Market, where a few local women display and sell their handcrafted hats, baskets, and other goods. Farther around the bend, past the impressive pink and white Government Administration Building and Hotel Peace and Plenty, the 150-year-old St. Andrew's Anglican Church faces west, its brilliant white walls and royal blue doors and shutters almost glowing in the bright afternoon sun.

By rented car or public bus, you can explore outward, north and south, from George Town. To the south is Rolle Town, with its old, vibrantly painted buildings and tiny bridge that links Great Exuma to Little Exuma. The small town of The Ferry affords wonderful views of the sea. It is the home of 70-year-old Gloria Patience, "the Shark Lady," who catches sharks, sells their meat, and makes shark's teeth jewelry, which is for sale in her museumlike house. Just farther south you can look out over Pretty Molly Bay from the now-closed Sand Dollar Beach Club, before proceeding to Williams Town, site of the Old Hermitage or "Cotton House," a nearly 200-year-old plantation estate. North of George Town, you drive through Jimmy Hill, notable for great expanses of deserted beach; Mt. Thompson, with its large bay and the shadeless white sand beach of Ocean Bight; and Steventon, before arriving at the charming hilltop village of Rolleville.

For snorkelers and divers, the Exumas offer a variety of underwater delights. The cays are surrounded by coral reefs at shallow and medium depths, and deeper wall diving reveals large formations of black coral. Blue holes, an uncharted Mystery Cave, and various banks and cays invite exploration. The scuba sites are abundant and the explorers few. Only in March and April, during the Cruising (or Crazy) Regatta and the Out Island Regatta, when festive visitors swamp George Town, is Great Exuma's languorous peace transformed into hectic plenty.

NOTEWORTHY

Stocking Island, about one mile offshore, protects Elizabeth Harbour from the Atlantic Ocean. Its miles of gorgeous, secluded beaches afford private sunbathing, excellent shelling, and marvelous swimming. (Some speculate that this may have been Christopher Columbus's first landing in the New World, a conjecture that San Salvadorans hotly dispute). Its isolation and pristine beauty make it an ideal one-day escape into remote paradise. Boat transportation is available at Hotel Peace and Plenty for $5 (free to the hotel's guests).

WHERE TO STAY

Peace and Plenty

P.O. Box 29055

George Town, Exuma, Bahamas

Telephone: (809) 336-2551; fax: (809) 336-2093

The oldest hotel in the Exumas, overlooking Elizabeth Harbour, was a sponge market until converted in the 1950s. Its distinctive pink-and-white painted buildings, with gabled roofs and dormer windows, add the charm needed to offset its size and tourist bustle. The popular hotel features 32 air-conditioned rooms (poolside, waterfront, or garden suites), a swimming pool, an attractive indoor-outdoor dining room, two cocktail lounges, twice-weekly dancing to live calypso, and courtesy boat transportation to Stocking Island. The lobby is a good place to glean information from bulletin boards and staff about what is happening in George Town. Rates are $78 to $85 for a double in the summer, $104 to $120 during the winter. A new facility with sixteen rooms and a bar/restaurant has been constructed on the beach one mile away. It's called Peace and Plenty West.

Two Turtles Inn

P.O. Box 29251

George Town, Exuma, Bahamas

Telephone: (809) 336-2545; fax: (809) 336-2528

Located across the street from the Straw Market, near the bend in the road at Elizabeth Harbour, Two Turtles is a small, woodsy, 12-room motel-style inn. The trade-offs for the clean but ordinary accommodations are the relatively reasonable rates and the lively, informal atmosphere. Locals and tourists gather at the outdoor bar and in the pleasant courtyard for often boisterous discussions of news and events. The restaurant, carved out of rock, serves excellent local seafood and native dishes for breakfast, lunch, and dinner, and the waitresses and cooks are very friendly. All of the rooms are air-conditioned, with ceiling fans and television. Rates are $68 in summer, $88 in winter, with four kitchenettes available at $78 and $98. Rates include use of an all-terrain Jeep, moped, or bicycle.

Pirate's Point Villas
P.O. Box 23
George Town, Exuma, Bahamas
Telephone: (809) 336-2554
Three comfortable housekeeping villas located on a private beach. Each rents for $90 a day, or $550 per week.

Marshall's Guest House
P.O. Box 27
George Town, Exuma, Bahamas
Telephone: (809) 336-2571
These very simple island accommodations—12 rooms in a plain building off the beach in town—are fine for the budget traveler at $24 single and $38 double.

RESTAURANTS

All the Great Exuma hotels have good restaurants that serve different combinations of Bahamian, American, and international cuisine in attractive dining areas. For very inexpensive home-cooked native meals, check out Liz 'n' Jim's, a tiny, weathered shanty in George Town. Darville's Supplies sells good homemade cakes and breads.

HOW TO GET THERE

Bahamasair has regularly scheduled service into George Town from Nassau. But be sure to recheck on all flights, as they are occasionally rerouted through Deadman's Cay, depending on the number of potential passengers; or, as one woman put it, "With this flight you take your chances. They should have told you."

PRACTICAL TIPS

Immigration: U.S. citizens do not need a passport or visa to visit the Bahamas for periods not exceeding eight months; a birth certificate or voter registration card is accepted as proof of citizenship, along with a photo I.D. There is a $10 airport departure tax.

Currency: The Bahamian dollar is held on an exact par with the U.S. dollar. Both currencies are used throughout the Bahamas.

TURKS AND CAICOS

The Turks and Caicos have long been called the "forgotten islands." One hour and 20 minutes southeast of Miami by jet, this British Crown Colony consists of eight small islands and 40 small cays, with a total population of 14,000 citizens scattered among the eight inhabited islands. Even with increasing development as a tourist destination, there is still about one mile of private beach for each inhabitant! Part of the Bahamas chain, the Turks and Caicos are flat islands with magnificent, empty beaches and the finest diving sites in the world. Inside the spectacular continuous coral reef, underwater visibility often reaches 200 feet. There are five bird sanctuaries, 13 national parks, and nine nature preserves.

The inhabited Caicos Islands include Providenciales (with direct air service to Miami), North Caicos, Middle Caicos, East Caicos, Pine Cay, and South Caicos. Across a 22-mile deep-water channel lie Grand Turk and Salt Cay in the Turks group.

Providenciales

Of all the Turks and Caicos islands, Providenciales (known locally as "Provo") offers the visitor the widest choice of hotel accommodations, restaurants, and stores without spoiling its tranquil and friendly atmosphere. It is an island of peaceful rolling hills, a natural deep harbor, flowering cactus, and a spectacular coral reef for snorkeling, swimming, and diving. Our return visit found condominium developments, a 228-room Ramada hotel, a golf course and casino. True escapists should head directly for the outer islands.

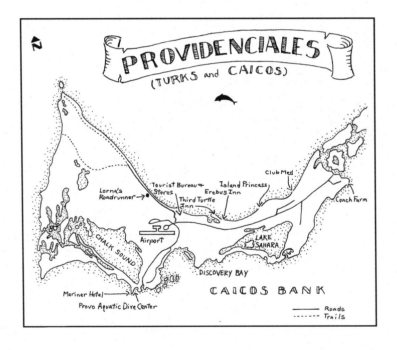

Pine Cay

Pine Cay is one of a chain of islets connecting Providenciales and North Caicos. Two miles long and covering 800 acres, it is a small, private residential community but run as a nature preserve, with a 12-room hotel. For the traveler who does not have to ask the price, the small and comfortable Meridian Club provides the ultimate escape from the rigors of the 20th century. The two-mile beach is one of the finest in the Caribbean, and, of course, it is never crowded. There is a freshwater pool, tennis court, windsurfing, a nature trail featuring a wide variety of birds and plants, and outstanding snorkeling, diving, and fishing.

Rates start at $395 per couple and include three meals a day, free use of sailboats, bicycles, and snorkeling gear, boating excursions to neighboring islands, and free postage stamps! Closed July through October.

NOTEWORTHY

Fort George Cay National Park: Off the north coast of Pine Cay are ruins of a British fort. With the help of a local guide, traces of pre-Columbian settlements can be found in this unique park.

Water Cay and Little Water Cay: Off the south coast, these tiny islands are a shell collector's dream.

WHERE TO STAY

Meridian Club
Pine Cay, Turks and Caicos, British West Indies
Reservations: U.S. telephone: (800) 331-9154;
fax: (212) 689-1598

RESTAURANTS

On Pine Cay, the only food available is served at the Meridian Club.

HOW TO GET THERE

The hotel makes arrangements to meet you at the Providenciales airport for a short hop to the island.

North Caicos

Nature lovers will find an earthly paradise on North Caicos, population 1,305. This large and most northerly of the chain is also the most fertile. Limes, papayas, sapodillas, oranges, tamarinds, and grapefruit abound. Endless beautiful beaches ring the island. Charming villages, quiet walks, and unusual species of birds are among its wonders.

NOTEWORTHY

Flamingo Pond, to the south of Whitby, harbors a nesting place for exotic flamingos, now rare in the wild.

Bottle Creek Settlements: Six miles southeast of Whitby, this quiet settlement has changed little since the 19th century. Inhabitants live mainly off fresh fish, crayfish, and shellfish. Beautiful beaches offer long, solitary walks and swims in the crystal clear water.

Four miles west of Whitby by boat, Three Mary Cays is a haven of unspoiled beauty, fine beaches and clear water; it is home to the now-endangered osprey.

Handicrafts: North Caicos is the center of basket making in the islands; several women here are considered to be experts in their field.

WHERE TO STAY

Pelican Beach Hotel
Whitby
North Caicos, Turks and Caicos, British West Indies
Telephone: (809) 946-7112; fax: (809) 946-7114
North Caicos native Clifford Gardiner owns and operates this friendly 12-room and two-suite hotel. Daily rates start at $68 per person and include breakfast and dinner. There are ten miles of uncrowded white sand beach at your doorstep. Equipment is available for day sailing, snorkeling, and scuba.

Prospect of Whitby Hotel
North Caicos, Turks and Caicos, British West Indies
Telephone: (809) 946-7119; fax: (809) 946-7114
Situated on a seven-mile-long stretch of beach, the 28-room Prospect of Whitby Hotel provides a swimming pool, tennis, dive shop, and water sports. Fresh produce comes from their garden. This renovated luxury hotel has been leased to an Italian company and most of the guests are Italian. Viva Italia!

Joanne's Bed and Breakfast
Whitby Beach
North Caicos, Turks and Caicos, British West Indies
Telephone and fax: (809) 946-7301
Set back from the beach, the rooms are light and airy with

wonderful views. The daily rate is $80 per room. Also available are two nearby housekeeping apartments.

RESTAURANTS

There are now four small, local cuisine restaurants on North Caicos: Green Village Restaurant; Titter's (live entertainment Fridays); Super D Café; and Wendy's at Bottle Creek.

HOW TO GET THERE

There are regular 15-minute flights from Providenciales to North Caicos on Turks and Caicos National Airways. U.S. telephone: (800) 845-2161 for current schedules and reservations.

Middle Caicos

With a population of only 300 residents, Grand Caicos, or Middle Caicos as it is often called, is the largest and least developed of any of the inhabited Turks and Caicos. This attractive island, with magnificent beaches and beautiful scenery, is also the most interesting. For the adventurous traveler interested in archaeology and geology, Middle Caicos is a veritable untrodden paradise. Along the northern coast, towering limestone cliffs drop sharply to placid, white, secluded beaches. These bluffs offer a dramatic panorama seldom experienced on other subtropical islands.

Conch Bar is the largest of three settlements and the location of several guest houses and the airplane runway. Nearby are barely explored, cathedral-sized caves where Lucayan Indian artifacts have recently been discovered. The caves are impressive: pure white stalactites and mysterious underground salt lakes. Several of the entrances to the different caves are slightly hidden by large calcite pillars, while some are underwater. Once the entrances are located, however, there is no difficulty finding the various chambers.

Between the villages of Bambarra and Lorimer are the interesting ruins of a settlement of Arawak and Lucayan Indians. Two miles south is Big Pond, a rich and varied plant and animal life reserve.

At Maria Taylor's four-room guest house in Conch Bar Settlement, visitors are greeted by some of the most hospitable inhabitants of these islands. Arrangements can be made for island excursions or bonefishing, or they can point you in the right direction for excellent beachcombing and shelling among the secluded hideaways on the northern coast.

WHERE TO STAY

Maria Taylor's Guest House
Conch Bar Settlement
Middle Caicos, Turks and Caicos, British West Indies
Telephone: (809) 946-3322
Daily room rate is $40.

Arthur Guest House
Middle Caicos, Turks and Caicos, British West Indies
Telephone: (809) 946-6122
Dolphus and Statia Arthur have appointed their three rooms with fans and cooking facilities. The beach is nearby.

Sea View Guest House
Middle Caicos, Turks and Caicos, British West Indies
Telephone: (809) 946-6117
The guest house comprises four rooms with fans and a local-style restaurant.

Eagle Rest Villas

Middle Caicos, Turks and Caicos, British West Indies
Telephone: (809) 946-2142; U.S. telephone: (215) 255-4640
Daily rates for these housekeeping units start at $110, $770
weekly.

RESTAURANTS

Carey's Restaurant and Bar, located on Seaview Street,
serves local dishes for lunch and dinner. Darts and domi-
noes are part of the scene.

Photo by Derk Richardson

Lush vegetation grows on the island

HOW TO GET THERE

There are several daily 35-minute flights from Providenciales to Middle Caicos on Turks and Caicos Airways.

Photo by Burl Willes

Underwater life on Middle Caicos

South Caicos

South Caicos Island, population 1,220, has long been an important export-oriented fishing center. Along the west coast, the shallow water of the Caicos Bank is the home of the single most important industry: the harvesting and export of conch and spiny lobster. The island's four blast-freeze plants process more than 750,000 pounds of lobster for export annually.

But South Caicos is far from spoiled by its industry. The southern coast offers outstanding diving and beautiful white sand beaches. The scuba diver will delight in the multitude and variety of marine life. Loggerhead turtles, barracudas, spotted eagle rays, octopuses, grouper, and snapper abound. This area is also well known for the huge wall-growing sponges that reach lengths of 100 to 150 feet.

Cockburn Harbour, the main settlement, is the best natural harbor in the Caicos Islands and provides good protection for yachts in almost any weather. Here you will find grocery stores, a clinic, a telephone station, and overnight accomodations. A good view of Cockburn Harbour can be enjoyed from Highlands, a 19th-century house.

WHERE TO STAY

Club Carib Harbour Hotel
Cockburn Harbour
South Caicos, Turks and Caicos, British West Indies
Telephone: (809) 946-3444; fax: (809) 946-3446
One-, two-, and three-bedroom oceanfront suites start at $70.

Corean's Cottage
Cockburn Harbour
South Caicos, Turks and Caicos, British West Indies
Telephone: (809) 946-3285
There are seven rooms with fans in this reasonably priced guest house.

RESTAURANTS

Local cuisine restaurants include Muriel's, Love's, Eastern Inn Restaurant and Bar, Café Columbus, Hayden's Place, and Myrna-Lisa's.

HOW TO GET THERE

There are daily 20-minute flights from Providenciales to South Caicos on Turks and Caicos National Airways and Inter Island Airways.

Salt Cay

Just five minutes by air from Grand Turk, Salt Cay is a peaceful, quiet, and colorful island with a magnificent beach bordering the north coast. The windmills that once powered the salt industry add an exotic touch to the landscape and 19th-century architecture. Whale watching is a memorable experience from January through March.

In his newsletter "The Plantation," Guy Lovelace writes:

Recent studies reveal that many of the usual things tourists have come to expect as a part of their Caribbean vacation are nowhere to be found on Salt Cay.

Prominent travel experts report that they have been unable to find more than four automobiles. There are no paved roads, no beach vendors, casinos or discos. There is little rainfall and as a result of this failure there are no mosquitoes or sand fleas.

A diligent search of court records reveals no crime, the most recent conviction resulted four years ago when one of the local men was caught in the dastardly act of riding his bicycle at night without a light.

There are no unfriendly local people. If local people can be found at all on a walk around the island they will be delighted to tell you about their gardens or fishing. Local people may be hard to find as there are only 190 on the island, one-half of which are children.

WHERE TO STAY

Mount Pleasant Guest House
Salt Cay, Turks and Caicos, British West Indies
Telephone and fax: (809) 946-6927
Simple accommodations and renowned native dishes are featured at this seven-room guest house, a friendly home away from home. Rates are $65 for a single, $85 for a double. Weekly dive packages are available. Locals on neighboring Grand Turk say Mount Pleasant has one of the best kitchens in the islands.

The Windmills at Salt Cay
Salt Cay, Turks and Caicos, British West Indies
U.S. telephone: (800) 822-7715; fax: (809) 946-6962
Patricia and Guy Lovelace provide a warm welcome at their small and very comfortable hotel, where rooms and suites face a superb two-mile stretch of beach. The daily rate of $490 for two sharing a room includes three meals, all beverages (including an open bar), transfers, island tour and boat trip/picnic to a deserted island, and gratuities.

Guests booking six nights directly with the hotel have their airfare paid from Providenciales to Salt Cay.

RESTAURANTS

On Salt Cay, the only food available is served at your guest house or hotel.

HOW TO GET THERE

There are flights seven days a week from Providenciales to Salt Cay on Turks and Caicos Airways (flying time is 20 minutes). From Grand Turk the flight is just five minutes.

Photo courtesy of Trombone Associates

Old salt warehouse, Salt Cay

Grand Turk

Divers are often the first visitors to discover an unspoiled island. That certainly is the case with Grand Turk, a six-mile-long British colony with a flat, sandy coastline and 19th-century capital at Cockburn Town. Flying in on an eight-passenger TAC National plane, I could see the dive boats moored along the coast.

While the divers had obviously come for the island's offshore attractions, this was also an island to enjoy by foot or bike. The buildings facing the sea along Front Street were in a charming weathered state, reflecting their age and endurance. On a narrow side street, horses grazed on the dry lawn of an abandoned house. This sleepy, endearing town has just enough amenities for comfort, without spoiling its 19th-century colonial past. Tiny restaurants, some with just one table, occupied the boat houses along the sea.

The solar salt pans started by settlers from Bermuda once brought wealth and prosperity to Grand Turk, inspiring the construction of a number of fine buildings and churches: Waterloo House (1815), now the governor's res-

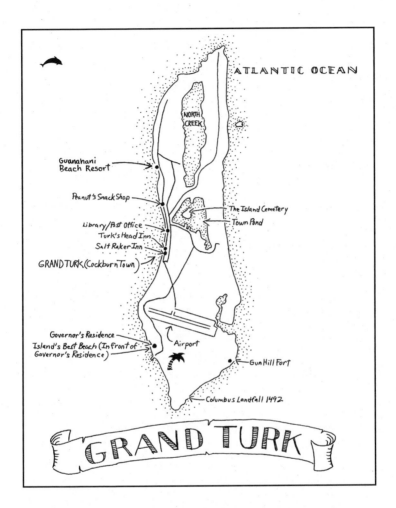

idence; a Victorian library; and an attractive wood-and-limestone Government House, which is still the colony's administrative center.

Facing the beach near town, the 150-year-old main house of Salt Raker Inn looked inviting. Once I saw the rear garden and attractive open air dining area, I knew I would be settling in for a while. The manager unlocked one of the garden sheds and presented me with a bicycle. I was off in a flash to explore this quiet, friendly island.

NOTEWORTHY

Swimming: Governor's Beach, only a ten-minute bicycle ride from town, offers excellent swimming and snorkeling.

Scuba: The diving on Grand Turk is superb. The 6,000-foot-deep underwater "Grand Canyon" of coral is one of the natural wonders of the world. The diving instructors are excellent and will point out incredible marine creatures, purple tube sponges, and black coral.

Bird-watching: Gibb and Round Cay Bird Sanctuaries are home to many interesting species.

Music: Ask around town for ripsaw music. Music on Grand Turk is informal and noncommercial.

Camping: No public camping facilities are provided in the islands; however, camping is permitted. It is recommended that you contact local police or the island magistrate, stating your intentions and the proposed location of your campsite.

Good Buys: For less than a dollar, one can buy a handful of fascinating Turks and Caicos stamps. A series of 18th-century boats makes a fine gift, either framed or laminated as a bookmark. The post office is easy to find on Front Street, next to the government offices.

Museum: The Turks and Caicos National Museum is located on the waterfront in the restored Guinep House. Artifacts reflect the island's rich cultural diversity, and its

central exhibit tells the story of the oldest shipwreck discovered in the Americas. Telephone: (809) 946-2166.

WHERE TO STAY

Turks Head Inn
P.O. Box 58
Grand Turk, Turks and Caicos, British West Indies
Telephone: (809) 946-62466; fax: (809) 946-2825
Located in an old garden with towering trees, this roman-
tic 150-year-old inn has a split-level covered veranda and
four-poster beds. Sue and Xavier Tonneau purchased and
nicely renovated it since our last visit. There are six rooms
with private bath and air conditioning, balcony, and view.
The $85 rate for two includes tax and breakfast.

Salt Raker Inn
Duke Street
Grand Turk, Turks and Caicos, British West Indies
Telephone: (809) 946-2260; fax: (809) 946-2817
The informal 150-year-old main house is of Bermudian architecture and includes three large, airy suites overlooking
the sea at the Salt Raker's own beach. Owner/innkeeper
Jenny Smith has upgraded each economy room with ceramic tile, a fridge, and air conditioning. In the lodge you
will find a well-stocked library, maps, and travel information. Rates start at $95 for two. The excellent kitchen and
live music bring out the locals on Wednesday and Sunday
evenings.

Coral Reef Beach Club

Grand Turk, Turks and Caicos, British West Indies
Telephone: (809) 946-2055; fax: (809) 946-2911
This beachfront resort on the island's east side has 21 units,
a freshwater pool, lighted tennis court, modern gym, and
Jacuzzi. The rate for a one-bedroom apartment is $90.

Guanahani Beach Resort

Grand Turk, Turks and Caicos, British West Indies
Telephone: (809) 946-2135; fax: (809) 946-1460
After visiting many Caribbean islands, Canadians Sheila and
Bryan Boundey decided, "Grand Turk's the one!"

"The island is so quaint and quiet and the people are
friendly and warm," Sheila explained. "You can take a walk
by yourself at midnight and there is no problem."

The Boundeys returned in August 1994 to manage this
16-room hotel on a three-mile white sand beach. Rooms
have two double beds and balconies that face west for
spectacular sunsets. Rates are $75 per night.

RESTAURANTS

Directly on the beach at the north of Front Street, Peanuts
Snak Shop has but one table and a few benches. The
friendly owner, Peanuts Butterfield, cooks delicious conch
fritters on her little outdoor gas burner. Ask to see her
family photo album.

Diners at Turks Head Inn enjoy consistently good
food, especially the fish dishes. There is outdoor dining on
the new veranda at the Salt Raker Inn and casual, excellent
local dishes (especially conch) at the Regal Beagle.

HOW TO GET THERE

There is regular air service to Grand Turk, from Miami via Providenciales, on Turks and Caicos Airways. U.S. telephone: (800) 845-2161.

PRACTICAL TIPS

Immigration: U.S. citizens need a passport or proof of citizenship with a photo I.D. All visitors must have an on-going or return ticket. Departure tax is $15.

Currency: The unit of currency is the U.S. dollar.

Health: Avoid tap water on Grand Turk, Salt Cay, and South Caicos. Dress: Casual and informal, but no swimsuits in public places.

PUERTO RICO'S ISLANDS

Over the past decade, a few selective travelers have discovered the secluded delights of two relatively unknown Puerto Rican islands, Vieques and Culebra. Visited by Columbus on his second New World voyage in 1493 and once known as the Spanish Virgin Islands, these two small islands are only a few miles off the east coast of Puerto Rico, but they remain essentially undiscovered by tourists. Throughout most of the 20th century, they have been under the jurisdiction of the United States. From 1901, Culebra was the site of a naval reservation, and from World War II through the mid-1970s, the island was used for U.S. Navy gunnery and bombing practice. There is no longer a military presence on Culebra. In 1948, the navy took possession of two-thirds of the land on Vieques, and while both the navy and marines maintain training bases on the island, much of the land has been leased for cattle grazing. The sailors and marines seem to have a minimal impact on life on Vieques, although their presence is still an object of native protest. The populations of both Culebra and Vieques have grown in the past decade, after a precipitous decline caused by military maneuvers. Now the two islands are characterized by an easygoing social atmosphere to complement the splendid weather, beautiful geography, and relaxing pace.

Photo by Derk Richardson

Sun Bay

Vieques

Driving from the tiny airport on the north coast of Vieques through the four miles of rolling hills to Esperanza, located on the south side of the island where most vacationers stay, the unique appeal of this Puerto Rican island begins to reveal itself. Cattle graze contentedly on the scrubby hillsides, accompanied by the lanky, white African egrets that keep them free of insects. Arching expanses of white beach flash into view through lush foliage. Sunlight filters through palm, mango, and flamboyant trees, dappling the roadway with dazzling patterns of shadow and light. A mere six miles from the east end of Puerto Rico, Vieques is light-years removed from the frantic pace of modern civilization. This 51-square-mile island (21 miles long and one to five miles wide) boasts some of the most beautiful beaches in the Caribbean and a way of life that harkens back to another century.

Once the home of 25,000 Spanish-speaking people, Vieques was a major sugar-producing island. None of the four sugar mills remains today, however, and the population is down to about 8,000, most of whom depend on cattle farming, fishing, and light industry for their livelihood. Most natives live in the central section of the island, between the eastern and western U.S. military reserves. The chief town is Isabel Segunda, on the northern side, with about 3,500 residents. But most visitors stay near Esperanza, a strip of beach with a new promenade on the southern coast. Vieques was used as a location for the films *Lord of the Flies* and *Heartbreak Ridge*, but the island is noted far more for its magnificent beaches and abundant wildlife, including birds, lizards, crabs, mongooses, and wild *paso fino* (fine-gait) horses. The temperature seldom varies much from 80 degrees F year-round, with refreshing breezes blowing in from the sea, and rainfall averaging only 47 inches per year. Diving, snorkeling, and nighttime trips to the spectacular Phosphorescent Bay are available through Sharon Graso at La Casa (741-3751).

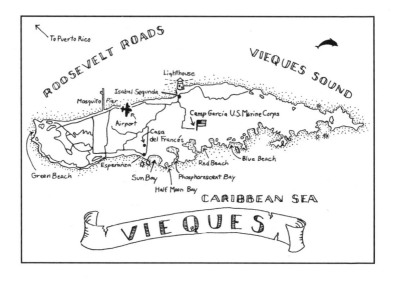

Getting around the island is remarkably easy, whether or not you rent a jeep, car, motor scooter, or bicycle. The public vans (*públicos*) will pick you up and drop you off anywhere on their route for one dollar, and for a negotiated fee they will become taxis, taking you wherever you like. Once you are in Esperanza or Isabel Segunda, everything is within walking distance.

One of our favorite walks was from Sun Bay, near Esperanza, to Media Luna and Navia. For much of the morning, we were the only swimmers on the vast expanse of beach at Sun Bay. Walking along the road that winds around to Media Luna, we encountered mongooses and several of the island's small wild horses. Although there were signs of previous visitors to this sheltered bay, once again we were alone on the beach. Continuing to Navia, we finally encountered a "crowd," about six other people on the long strip of white sand. We spent the rest of the afternoon watching the sand crabs dart in and out of their holes and napping in the softening afternoon sunshine, lulled by the sounds of the breeze and surf.

The island of Vieques is not all that remote—being so easily accessible from Puerto Rico—but with its many secluded beaches, scattered population, and light tourist trade, it has all the advantages of being off the beaten track.

NOTEWORTHY

You could spend weeks just exploring the many beaches of Vieques, and all are worth investigating.

Sun Bay is a mile-and-a-half-long, crescent-shaped beach in a public park just east of Esperanza. Coconut palms line the shore, providing ample shade. The one- to two-foot waves are just high enough to make swimming interesting. The government maintains the beach, parking lot, picnic tables, and bathhouse, but a "crowd" might amount to a dozen people on the entire beach. Admission is $2 per car.

Media Luna ("Half Moon") is a small enclosed beach farther to the east from Sun Bay. Here you can wade out 100 yards or more in warm, absolutely still water.

Navia (also called "Third Beach"), beyond Media Luna, is one of the most beautiful on the island. Waves roll in from the ocean past a rocky promontory, and sand crabs dash in and out of their holes in the beach.

Green Beach, at the western end of Vieques, is acces-

Photo by Derk Richardson

Long, empty Green Beach

sible with a day pass through the naval reservation. It is long, empty, and gorgeous, affording a finé view back to Puerto Rico.

Isabel Segunda, the main population center of Vieques, was founded in 1843 and is worth a morning or afternoon of exploration. A deserted lighthouse built in 1896 rises 68 feet above the harbor. High on the hill behind town, El Fortin, a restored 145-year-old Spanish fort (the last one constructed in the New World), allows a grand view of the city and the northern coastline.

WHERE TO STAY

Casa del Francés
P.O. Box 458
Vieques, Puerto Rico 00765
Telephone: (809) 741-3751
Irving Greenblatt, a cantankerous retired businessman from Boston, runs what many people consider to be "the only place to stay" on Vieques. His hotel is a revamped turn-of-the-century French sugar plantation, sitting on a hill above Esperanza. The downstairs rooms have 17-foot ceilings and open out onto sunny verandas. Not all rooms are equally spacious or ideally located. Meals are served in a classically "tropical," partially open dining room overlooking the cloistered swimming pool, and evening socializing revolves around a charming outdoor bar, surrounded by lush garden foliage. Irving is one of the island's most notable characters, and his staff takes good care of the Casa guests, many of whom return year after year. But the marvelous old building itself is showing distressing signs of

disrepair and will soon need the kind of serious attention that Irving puts into creating atmosphere. Rates in the summer season (April 30 to December 1) are $80; in winter, (December 1 to April 30), $95. Note: $30 per person is added for continental breakfast and dinner.

Posada Vista Mar
P.O. Box 495
Vieques, Puerto Rico 00765
Telephone: (809) 741-8716 or 8719
The best bargain, the most gracious hospitality, and the finest native cooking are available at this humble guest house on a low hill beyond the west end of Esperanza. An unbelievably thoughtful native Vieques woman named Olga rents out a half dozen small and clean but spartan rooms behind her screened-in restaurant. The sounds of crickets and the island's famous tree frogs (*coqí*) create a vibrant chorus at night, and the bleating of Olga's goats combines with the crowing of roosters in the early morning. Rates are $35 single or double. Olga also has an apartment available for longer rentals.

The Trade Winds
P.O. Box 1012
Vieques, Puerto Rico 00765
Telephone: (809) 741-8666 or 8368
Owner/hosts Janet and Harry Washburn warmly welcome guests to their well-maintained guest house right across the road from the promenade and Esperanza Beach. The staff is especially friendly. Rooms 1, 2, and 3 have an upper level terrace. Rates are $40 single and $50 double.

Villa Esperanza
Calle Flamboyan
Esperanza, Vieques, Puerto Rico 00765
Telephone: (809) 741-8675
This ambitious parador, situated on the site of an old sugar plantation at the east end of Esperanza, has modern villa apartments in configurations that can be rented as one- or two-bedroom units, but there are no kitchens. The closest thing to a resort on Vieques, Villa Esperanza features a restaurant, tennis courts, scooter and jeep rentals, and private beach access. Rates are $95 double.

New Dawn's Caribbean Retreat and Guest House
P.O. Box 1512
Vieques, Puerto Rico 00765
Telephone: (809) 741-0495
Located on a rural five-acre hillside overlooking the Caribbean, this women-built retreat is available by reservation to individuals, or families, as well as for group meetings or workshops. Rooms are $35 a day; a tent site (you bring the tent) is $10. You can rent the entire retreat for $350 a day (the price of one room at most luxury Caribbean resorts). The price goes down to $1,000 per week from May 15 to December 15—a bargain $85 per week, per person. Breakfast and dinner are available on request for an extra $15 per person.

RESTAURANTS

Posada Vista Mar offers superb and inexpensive native cuisine, specializing in fried whole fish—grouper or snapper—served with rice and *arepas* (sweet or savory fried dough).

El Queñepo, across the street from the beach at Esperanza, is operated by the garrulous Mario, a former Brooklyn resident who returned to Vieques and now prepares all varieties of seafood—crab, fish, lobster, octopus, conch—specializing in soups and salads, as well as entrées. For lunch, a meal of black beans, rice, and arepas is perfect.

Bananas is the "hot spot" at Esperanza, attracting what young tourist crowd there is to its outdoor bar facing the

Photo by Derk Richardson

The popular Bananas Restaurant in Esperanza

beach. It is especially popular with those who want a taste of such American standards as burgers, chili, and pizza, and it offers the most active nightlife on the weekends. Bananas also has several very basic rooms for rent in back.

The Trade Winds boasts the best ocean view from its attractive restaurant and bar, to go along with its popular lunch and dinner menus of creative meat and seafood dishes.

FROM MY JOURNAL

The goats are grazing outside our window at the Posada Vista Mar. Cocks are crowing throughout the neighborhood, helping us rise before dawn so we can catch the morning ferry to Fajardo. Olga taps gently at our door to make sure we're awake. In her little screened-in restaurant, she serves us coffee "on the house" and tells us what she knows about the neighboring Culebra. She says good-bye with a kiss on the cheek and a sincere wish that we will return someday.

HOW TO GET THERE

Isla Neña flies small planes to Vieques from San Juan's Isla Verde International Airport. Although these flights are theoretically scheduled for certain times, Isla Neña usually waits until they have three passengers before flying. Miguel or Marta staff the check-in desk next to U.S. Air. The fare is $40 one way. Telephone (809) 791-5110 for reservations.

Vieques Airlink flies from Isla Grande Airport, a 20-minute taxi ride from the International Airport. Telephone

(809) 722-3736 or 723-9882 for schedules and reservations.

A 400-passenger ferry leaves Fajardo, on the east coast of Puerto Rico, twice daily (9:00 a.m. and 4:30 p.m.) and arrives at the terminal in Isabel Segunda; the cost is $3 one way. Air Link and Flamenco fly in from Isla Grande Airport.

Público service is available from both the Vieques airport and Isabel Segunda to your destination on Vieques.

Culebra

At El Mini-Mas market in Central Dewey, Winnie and Virginia stand behind the counter and generously share stories and information about their island. They warn that in February and March the hotels and guest houses are "booked solid" (with about 100 vacationers). They recommend returning in April to watch thousands of sooty terns build their nests on the island's rocky ledges. They explain that the strange garden down the street—the one full of ceramic animals, painted truck tires, sea shells, and tortoise shells arranged into novel sculptures—belongs to "Cato," Winnie's aunt. They express their pleasure at the fact that few tourists come over from Puerto Rico, thus leaving their island to bask in its tranquil isolation. The unforced friendliness of Winnie and Virginia and the undisturbed natural wonders of Culebra that they describe are at the heart of this charming, unspoiled island's appeal.

On Puerto Rico and even on nearby Vieques, most people tell you that there is "nothing to do" on Culebra. They could not be further off the mark. A national wildlife refuge, mangrove forests, spectacular beaches, a sheltered deep-water bay, and extensive coral reefs are among the attractions, complemented by the warm hospitality of the nearly 2,000, mostly English-speaking residents. The 11-square-mile island, located 19 miles east of Puerto Rico, is the largest of 24 islands and cays that make up a small-scale archipelago. Culebra is teeming with wildlife, including sea turtles, giant lizards, and more than 85 species of birds. Its rolling hills, rising to gentle 300-foot peaks, invite exploration on foot or bicycle.

The human population, mostly descended from Spanish settlers, is centered in the small, sleepy town of Dewey

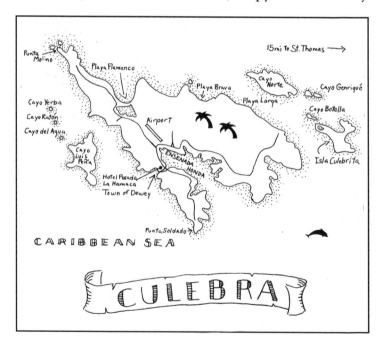

(known locally as "Puebla"), located on beautiful Ensenada Honda ("deep bay"). About 300 Culebrans work at the pharmaceutical equipment manufacturing company in Dewey, and most others, including several dozen transplanted North Americans and Europeans, are self-employed in services or fishing. Full employment and social harmony keep the island crime-free and wonderfully relaxed. Although the architecture of Dewey is unremarkable, barely reflecting the island's Spanish origins, the town is nonetheless attractive, with an impressive government building, interesting churches, a charming post office, an irresistible bakery, and pastel-colored houses packed close together on narrow streets. Culebra would seem ripe for development, and the number of cars and trucks on the roads is indeed surprising. But the island's reliance on rainwater, gathered in rooftop cisterns, and the preservation of lands in the National Refuge, restrict the rate and scope of growth. Private homes for vacationers and retirees continue to be built outside Dewey, but large-scale tourist development seems unlikely. One of the small pleasures on Culebra is to look up and see the airplanes carrying tourists from San Juan to St. Thomas, only 14 miles away, and know that most of the passengers will not even notice the undiscovered island below.

NOTEWORTHY

Playa Flamenco, on the north coast, is the most spectacular of Culebra's many fine beaches. The surf can be rough, but it does not inhibit swimming, and you are likely to find yourself the sole visitor on nearly a mile of clean, white sand.

Culebrita (like Cayo Luis Peña) is a large cay that is

Puerto Rico Tourist Bureau

The beach of Playa Flamenco

part of the wildlife refuge and home to the endangered hawksbill turtle. The nearby mile-long coral formation is one of the finest diving and snorkeling spots in the region. Culebra's offshore cays can be reached by hiring a local fishing boat or sailboat.

Mount Resaca comprises a large piece of the refuge land on the northern side of Culebra. It is marked by sections of dry subtropical forest, with the fascinating vegetation including thorn thickets, palms, and cactus. The huge boulder formations support beautiful varieties of orchids, bromeliads, and peperomia.

Johanna's Fantasy Island, tucked away in a remote mangrove swamp, is the dream hideaway of Johanna Taylor, who built her own home in the exotic tangle of mangrove roots. A hired boat can carry you up to her dock, and if she is home, Johanna comes out and offers 25-cent tours, including the jewelry and souvenirs that she crafts by hand.

WHERE TO STAY

Posada La Hamaca
P.O. Box 186
Culebra, Puerto Rico 00775
Telephone: (809) 742-3516
The neat and clean but somewhat stark accommodations include six hotel rooms upstairs and three efficiency units downstairs, each with its own bath. Located in Dewey on the canal leading to Ensenada Honda, this friendly hotel features an "honor bar" and barbecue on the canal-side patio, and van transportation to Flamenco Beach. Rates start at $50 double.

Club Seabourne

Fulladosza Road
Culebra, Puerto Rico 00775
Telephone: (809) 742-3169; fax: (809) 742-3176
About a mile or so outside Dewey, the Seabourne is situated on a hillside with a fine view of Ensenada Honda. A spectacular flower garden slopes up to the swimming pool, screened outdoor dining room, and patio bar. The Seabourne offers rooms starting at $90 per night, double; air-conditioned rooms and cottages at $100 per night per couple. Rates include continental breakfast and transportation to and from the airport or ferry terminal.

Coral Island Guest House

Box 396
Culebra, Puerto Rico 00775
Telephone: (809) 742-3177
Located across the street from the ferry terminal, this simple hotel offers rooms for $45 daily and complete apartments with kitchens for $125. Some rooms have balconies overlooking the harbor and town, but this is a very basic spot, probably best for people who will spend most of their time enjoying such water sports as windsurfing, diving, and snorkeling. Bike rentals are $10 per day.

Weekly Rentals

A wide variety of fully furnished apartments, cottages, and houses are available for short- and long-term rentals. Full information can be provided by the Tourism Office, P.O. Box 189, Culebra, Puerto Rico 00775. Telephone: (809) 742-3291.

Cielo y Mar Guest House and Culebra Island Condos
Box 292
Culebra, Puerto Rico 00775
Telephone: (809) 742-3167
U.S. telephone for Culebra Island Condos: (201) 458-5591
Located out of town at Punta Aloe, overlooking Ensenada Honda, these are modern, fully equipped houses and apartments, with a vast array of amenities, appliances, and conveniences. They start at $400 off-season, for one to three people, and go up to $775 per week in peak season, for four to six people.

RESTAURANTS

El Pescador, in downtown Dewey, serves delicious island food, including shark empanadas, pimento rellenos, lobster soup, pastilillos, arepas, and flan, as well as steaks, chops, and pasta dishes. Louisa, the Brooklyn-born waitress, has lived in Culebra for 15 years and can share stories in her free moments.

Marta's "Al Fresco," in downtown Dewey close to the ferry landing, offers a variety of local seafood (marinated octopus is the house special) served either indoors, near the bar, or in an enclosed garden patio.

El Batay, located on the road leading out of town toward the airport, is a stark bar/pool room that serves delicious and inexpensive grilled sandwiches on locally baked bread.

Club Seaborne boasts the most elegant and most expensive ($15 to $20 range) dining on Culebra, with seafood and continental dishes prepared by a French cook and served in an attractive dining area overlooking beautiful Ensenada Honda.

FROM MY JOURNAL

The walk from Dewey to Punta Soldado winds past small houses and expansive estates along Ensenada Honda. Long brown pods hang from the trees along the road, and the seeds inside rustle in the wind like a child's rattle. The hills sloping down into the smaller bays cast great curving shadows as the sun lowers itself toward the horizon. The flowers in the Club Seabourne's immense garden are all in bloom—a rainbow of color as vibrant as the changing hues of the cloud-streaked sky at dusk. The walk to the point is long, but the views are wonderful.

HOW TO GET THERE

From the Puerto Rico mainland, twice-daily ferry service is provided from Fajardo (on the eastern end of the island, a two-hour drive from San Juan). Boats leave at 9:00 a.m. and 4:30 p.m. The fare is $3, and travel time is one hour.

Flamenco Airways flies out of the Isla Grande Airport in San Juan (20 minutes by taxi from the International Airport). The 30-minute flight costs about $40. Telephone (809) 725-7707 or 723-8110 for schedules and reservations. There is also less frequent air service from St. Thomas and Vieques.

PRACTICAL TIPS

Immigration: Vieques and Culebra are part of the Puerto Rican Commonwealth of the United States, so U.S. citizens need not clear customs or immigration when traveling to or from Puerto Rico. (However, there is still an agricultural inspection on departure.)

Currency: The U.S. dollar is official currency on Culebra and Vieques.

Language: Spanish is the official language, but almost everyone speaks English.

Photo by Derk Richardson

Waterfront scene near Dewey

LEEWARD ISLANDS

The Bottom

Saba

If all you ever did on Saba was fly in, land, and then take off again, you would have experienced one of the most exhilarating adventures in the Caribbean. Imagine an airstrip that looks like a small stretch of sidewalk. Place it at the tip of a green volcanic island that rises suddenly and dramatically out of the deep blue sea. At either end of the runway, rocky cliffs drop off precipitously to the water 130 feet below. And at one end, the edge of the strip abuts the mountainside. "Of course, we're gong to approach from the end that juts out over the water," you think, as your tiny twin-engine, ten-seat STOL (Short Take-Off and Landing) airplane circles out over the ocean. Then your pilot swings the plane around and your heart jumps into your throat. The plane is aimed directly at the side of the mountain! Your breath stops short and your knuckles turn white. The plane makes a quick bank to the left, and before you know it, there's the runway. "We can't land at that angle!" the voice in your head cries. But before you can gasp again, the plane has touched down and stopped, using less than half of the 1,300-foot airstrip.

After landing on one of the shortest runways in the world, you might think that little else on this tiny chunk of the Netherlands Antilles could measure up for excitement. But remarkably, what lies in store on this five-square-mile Dutch island is all uphill. When you clear customs in the picturesque cottagelike airport, Saban taxi vans are waiting to take you from Flat Point (indeed, virtually the only flat point on Saba) up the steep road through 19 serpentine curves, through Hell's Gate, to your destination in the equally accurately-named Windwardside, or over the mountain to The Bottom. Your driver will probably tell you how the road was handbuilt, without any machinery, over the course of 20 years, from 1940 to 1960; that prior to that time, all goods were carried from one side of the island to the other over a grueling series of steps; and that only recently have the stone walls and eroded sections of concrete begun to be rebuilt.

As the drive continues, you might have to pinch yourself to make sure that you are not dreaming up this fairy tale island. The buildings, painted pristine white with glossy green trim and brick-red roofs, look like they have been preserved and transplanted from some remote European Alpine village. The flowers hanging over the wall along the road create an eye-catching riot of color against the unbroken background of rich green foliage. And the views forward, up the mountain where misty clouds brush across the ridges, and back down the steep slopes and canyons to the sea, leave you as breathless as did your landing.

Before you have reached either of Saba's two main villages, Windwardside or The Bottom, your driver will have shared a wealth of information. Helpful tips and personal stories flow freely from most of the 1,000 black and white residents of Saba, one of the friendliest islands in the Caribbean. For instance, there is Carmen, who works as waitress and bartender at Scout's Place by night, drives her own taxi van during the day, and is building a new house on the hillside overlooking The Bottom. A native of Saba, she can relate a book full of family and local history. At the Around the Bend clothing shop in Windwardside, Frida Johnson told us how her father was the first Saban to drive a jeep, and she remembers the big event when a woman first drove on the island. What you do not learn during your

first few hours on Saba, you can glean from *Saba: The First Guidebook*, an indispensable, thorough, and chatty self-published booklet by Natalie and Paul Pfanstiehl (11 Annandale Road, Newport, R.I. 02840).

As you soon learn, Saba is known as "The Unspoiled Queen." Tourists have yet to discover this "green gumdrop" in significant numbers. The island's history, however, is marked by repeated discoveries and battles for sovereignty—between the Dutch, English, and French—with the Dutch taking final hold in 1816. Today Dutch is the official language, but everyone speaks English. The Sabans, mostly descended from the original settlers and African slaves, take great pride in their island, keeping it strikingly clean and tidy. But they take great joy in sharing it, as well.

What is there to do on a Caribbean island that rises so abruptly out of the sea that it has no beaches? The first thing is to explore the villages. Windwardside, on the ridge between Booby Hill and Mount Scenery, gives new depth to the adjective "charming." Stroll down narrow streets past the old churches and the graveyard, and wander through the handful of shops and stores: the Superette, the Island Craft Shop, and Big Rock Market. Browse through an eye-popping selection of colorful stamps at the post office (there are even more at the main post office in The Bottom). Pick up maps, postcards, and information at the tourist office. At night, the activity is concentrated at the Chinese restaurant; at Guido's, where dancing takes precedence on the weekends; and at Cousin's Bar. But the streets are quiet, and you are serenaded to sleep by crickets, frogs, and the wind rustling through broad palm leaves.

It takes about an hour to walk from Windwardside

down through St. John's and Crispeen to The Bottom, but if you wave for a ride, someone is sure to pick you up. (The taxi ride costs about $8.) In addition to several quaintly officious administrative buildings in The Bottom, you will find the Saba Artisan Foundation, selling the island's famous lacelike drawn needlework, T-shirts, and several varieties of Saba Spice, a sweet and potent homemade concoction of mulled 151-proof rum; Earl's Snack Bar, Saba's answer to fast food; the splendid little Corner View Bakery, selling breads, tarts, and johnnycake; Nicholson's Supermarket; and the best native cooking on the island at Queenie's Serving Spoon.

After exploring Saba's "civilization," try the walks to Fort Bay or Ladder Bay from The Bottom; up Booby Hill or to the Lookout from Windwardside; a botanical tour with Anna Keene; or up the challenging 1,064 steps of Mount Scenery to an elevation of nearly 3,000 feet. When you are ready for a swim, the lack of beaches is no obstacle. You can swim and snorkel off the pier at Fort Bay. If you scuba dive, you will quickly learn that Saba is one of the great unspoiled diving locales of the eastern Caribbean. Two diving facilities—Edward Arnold's Saba Deep and Joan and Lou Borque's Sea Saba—will assist you in exploring Saba's recently established Marine Park. Underwater visibility averages 75 to 125 feet, and at the two dozen or so dive spots, you will find towering walls and pinnacles, giant coral mounds, sea fans, sponges, dense schools of fish, and scores of crustaceans.

During our first afternoon and evening on Saba, we began to feel at home. After another day, we had caught on to the Saban courtesy of waving to everyone you meet on the road, and we made friends with Tipsy, the one-and-a-half-eared cat who jumps into your lap at Scout's Place. By the third day, we knew how hard it was going to be to leave this mountainous emerald paradise and how easy it would be to return.

NOTEWORTHY

The hike up Mount Scenery, via the 1,064 stone steps, is steep and arduous at times. Most hikers average about an hour and 20 minutes to the top. But along the way you are rewarded with breathtaking views of all the settlements. The vegetation assumes giant proportions in the near rainforest setting. I sat for nearly an hour at the top, staring across the sea at St. Eustatius (Statia) and watching the clouds form and blow over the island as the cold sea air hit the warm air rising from the land. A number of nature trails have been laid out in the elfin forest around Mount Scenery. A pamphlet about the trails is available from the tourist office, which can also arrange for guides to lead visitors on hikes.

The Saba Museum, located near Captain's Quarters in Windwardside, was established in honor of Harry Luke Johnson, whose dream it was to complete such a project. The memorabilia include antique furniture, glassware, tools, and photographs and clippings relating the 20th-century history of Saba.

WHERE TO STAY

Scout's Place

Windwardside, Saba, Dutch Caribbean
Telephone: (011) 599-462-205; fax: (011) 599-462-388
Scout's Place proves that paradise need not be expensive.
Dianna Medero manages five rooms and a homey one-
bedroom apartment. The gingerbread-trimmed main building commands a gorgeous view of the Caribbean, especially from the patio bar and outdoor dining room. Dianna
serves the island's best breakfast (bacon, eggs, thick slices
of homemade toast, juice, coffee, or tea) in a cozy inside
dining room off the kitchen. In the late morning several
locals and taxi drivers gather at the bar for coffee and conversation. The kitchen turns out hearty lunches and full-
course dinners. Rates are $85 double, with breakfast and
dinner included. (For a small extra charge, Dianna will prepare lobster on special order.)

Captain's Quarters

Windwardside, Saba, Dutch Caribbean
Telephone and fax: (011) 599-462-377
Perched on the verdant hillside below Scout's Place,
Captain's Quarters is a beautifully restored former sea captain's home. Its ten rooms are neatly furnished, some with
antique four-poster beds. The outdoor dining pavilion and
terrace bar are vital centers of social activity, as is the
swimming pool, unique among Saba's hotels. Full-course
dinners feature lobster, steak, poultry, or fish, and reservations are required. The hotel closes down for the month of
September for maintenance. Summer rates are $95 and

$120 double, plus room tax and service charge, with Modified American Plan available for $40 per person. Rates include continental breakfast.

Juliana's

Windwardside, Saba, Dutch Caribbean

Telephone: (011) 599-463-218; fax: (011) 599-462-389

Juliana and Franklin manage a group of charming guest rooms, a cottage, and an apartment, each with bath, balcony, and views of the sea, gardens, and mountain scenery. Rooms are modern and immaculate, with sun deck and recreation room for guests, and a new swimming pool. Rates are $70 single, $90 double in winter; $60 single and $80 double in summer. Cottage-$140 winter, $100 summer. Apartment-$125 winter, $95 summer.

Cranston's Antique Inn

The Bottom, Saba, Dutch Caribbean

Telephone: (011) 599-463-218; fax: (011) 599-463-203

Originally built as a government guest house for visiting officials, this restored two-story Victorian house came under private management in 1964. Mr. J.C. Cranston and his son Edward have gradually turned the old building into a charming inn. The rooms are furnished with antiques and locally handcrafted curtains and coverlets. The tropical garden bar is a favorite afternoon and evening watering spot in The Bottom, and the recently-completed dining gazebos provide romantic settings for meals. Rates are $95 double, breakfast included.

The Gate House

Hell's Gate, Saba, Dutch Caribbean

Telephone: (011) 599-462-416; fax: (011) 599-462-529

While keeping true to the local architecture, the Gate House is the newest addition to the island's accommodations. Set high in the mountain, the view is spectacular. Each of the six rooms is tastefully furnished in a bright Caribbean style. All have private baths, and two units include kitchens. The Gate House café offers breakfast and dinner. Summer rates are $60 single, $70 double, and only $10 more during high season. Prices include a continental breakfast.

House and Apartment Rentals

A variety of cottages, apartments, and houses in Hell's Gate, Windwardside, and Booby Hill are available for daily, weekly, and monthly rental, with rates approximately $45 per day, $300 per week, and $900 per month. The Saba Tourist Bureau maintains and publishes current listings. You can write to them at P.O. Box 527, Windwardside, Saba, Dutch Caribbean. (Allow two weeks for mail delivery.) Telephone: (011) 599-462-231; fax: (011) 599-462-350.

RESTAURANTS

Queenie's Serving Spoon: "I have heart like marshmallow," Queenie Simmons told us when she was explaining the list of names on the wall. They were local Sabans who had not yet paid for meals she prepared on credit. Queenie and her daughters, Verna and Connie, also have a magic touch with the best down-home West Indian cuisine on Saba. Located on a back street of The Bottom, Queenie's gaily painted and wildly decorated little café has eight tables beneath homemade crepe paper "fly-catchers." For lunch, Queenie serves enormous portions of chicken in her special peanut butter sauce, with rice, greens, and fresh french fries. Call ahead for dinner, and she will prepare curried goat, stuffed onion fish, muffin dumplings, and banana or pumpkin fritters. She makes a dark, powerful Saba Spice, as well. Her full-page typed receipts include the salutation, "So my loveing friends i am now thanking you all and please come back again be looking out for you all soon." The feeling is genuine—and mutual.

The Saba Chinese Bar and Restaurant, in Windwardside, is famous for its egg rolls, but then it has little competition. This Caribbean anomaly serves from an extensive menu of Cantonese food and selected local dishes. At night the bar often becomes crowded and raucous, and you can sometimes hear the music a block away.

Guido's, behind the post office and the library in Windwardside, serves made-to-order pizza all day. In the afternoon you can play a quiet game of darts, but at night the bar becomes a gathering spot for young Sabans and tourists, and the place jumps with dancers on the weekends.

FROM MY JOURNAL

How can an island without beaches be such a paradise? Maybe it's precisely because it has no beaches, no surfers slicing through the waves or body-beautiful sun worshipers draped all over the shoreline. The island has a real Old World feel; the villages are permanently settled into the mountains and the customs are settled into the people. This is their home, above all, and they welcome visitors more as guests in their home than as tourists in their "facilities." Lunch at Queenie's, undisturbed snorkeling near the pier, fresh lobster for dinner, and a breezy late night walk under a bright canopy of stars—what else is there?

HOW TO GET THERE

There is regular, direct air service from the U.S. to St. Martin. Windward Island Air (Winair) flies from St. Martin and St. Eustatius to Saba five or more times a day. The flights are often booked, so be sure to reconfirm and check in early. The flight to Saba takes 15 minutes, unless a stop is added at St. Eustatius.

"The Edge," a high-speed ferry, makes the one-hour trip from Phillipsburg, St. Martin to Fort Bay on Saba several times a week. For more information, telephone (011) 599-542-640.

PRACTICAL TIPS

Immigration: A valid passport, birth certificate, or alien registration card is required for entry, plus a return or onward transportation ticket. There is a $2 departure tax.

Currency: The official currency is the Antilles florin (or guilder), with an exchange rate of approximately 1.77 florins to the U.S. dollar. But U.S. currency is routinely accepted throughout the island.

Language: Saba's official language is Dutch, but everyone on the island speaks English.

Barbuda

Paradise sometimes appears in the most peculiar and unexpected settings. Flying from Antigua into its sister island of Barbuda, one looks down on a rather uninviting landscape of flat, scrubby terrain. No rolling hills, winding rivers, spectacular cliffs, or waterfalls beckon the airborne traveler descending to a forsaken-looking, water-bound patch of earth. But as the small plane eases down in a graceful arc toward the tiny landing strip at Codrington, the pink and white rim of the island starts to reveal Barbuda's very special story. For here, effectively removed from all the commercial trappings of a conventional Caribbean vacation, along the edge of 62 square miles of unremarkable land, are miles and miles of magnificent, unspoiled beaches—among the most beautiful and least exploited in the Caribbean, if not the world. Barbuda is so rich in sandy beaches that a sand exportation business sends the "excess" to larger Caribbean islands for construction and restoration of their more heavily touristed beaches. And yet only a few hundred visitors venture the 25 miles from Antigua each year to enjoy the breathtakingly idyllic pleasures of Barbuda's unspoiled coastal rim.

Also visible from the air are dark brown and gray patches that mottle the gorgeous azure blue sea surrounding the island. These are the shadows of coral reefs—acres of them that lie unexplored in Barbuda's shallow waters. So even before landing, you have glimpsed the unique appeal of this wonderfully undiscovered island.

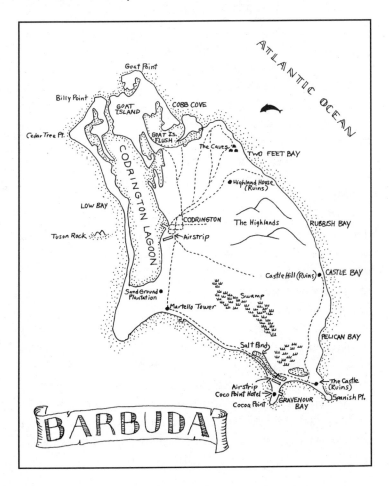

At the two-room Barbuda airport, a dozen or so people await the arrival of each plane. We were greeted by Sunset View Resort proprietor George (a.k.a. Profit) Burton, ready to recruit guests for his nearby hotel. Later in the morning, George loaded us into his truck and provided a tour of the island. The road was exceptionally rough, pitted with ruts and holes, but George seemed to know every inch. He pointed out a coconut plantation, the Martello Tower, and the sand-loading operation. He accompanied us to Coco Point, past a sign that warned the driver to watch for low-flying aircraft. Less than a mile north of Coco Point, he pulled his truck over to a slight opening in the dense brush and dropped us off at a gorgeous stretch of beach that we had to ourselves for the rest of the day. The sand was white and soft, and the calm waters had rock and coral formations within wading distance. Small fish circled around our ankles, practically playing tag with us as we swam. Like all the hosts on Barbuda, George Burton (one of many Barbudan Burtons) is a repository of information and tips, providing gracious hospitality and service to visitors. When we told him we had spotted a lobster underneath a rock ledge in the shallow waters, he told us we were "very lucky." Indeed, we were.

Barbuda is the "lesser" half of the two-island country Antigua-Barbuda, which gained its independence from Britain in 1983. Most of its 1,300 black residents live in Codrington, a rustic village situated on the southeast side of the large Western or Codrington Lagoon. Bird-watchers will be fascinated by the great variety of species that nest on the island, especially at the Frigate Bird Sanctuary, accessible by private boat. Hunters occasionally roam through the brush inland or around the island's salt ponds in pursuit of wild boar, deer, and duck. And if it is possible to tire of the absolute natural peace of sunning, swimming, and snorkeling at any of the white sand and dazzling pink, shell-laden beaches, there are many landmarks to investigate, such as the ruins of Sir William Codrington's Highland House estate, the Indian caves, or the Martello Tower, built by Spanish colonists as a beacon for ships at sea. Apparently, many seafarers did not spy the land in time, as some 60 or more ships have crashed and sunk in Barbuda's shallow, reef-bound waters. The wrecks provide fascinating excursions for scuba divers.

I discovered one of Barbuda's most interesting social phenomena during a walk through Codrington at dusk. As George Burton later explained, every morning the village residents open their gates and let their small herds of goats roam and graze freely around the island. Around such public buildings as the school and government house, the goats mow the wild grass into neat, closely cropped lawns. As sunset approaches, the goats migrate back to town in herds 100 or more strong. Once they reach the streets of Codrington, they break off into smaller groups and walk confidently through the neighborhood to find their own yard. It is an enlightening and moving experience to walk through the droves of tame, bleating goats as they are instinctively returning home. Once night falls, so does the level of activity in Codrington. This is not a tourist town. There are no souvenir shops or nightclubs, no dive shops or T-shirt concessions—just an eminently free and easy lifestyle for self-sufficient travelers who want to discover the best secluded Caribbean spots for themselves.

NOTEWORTHY

Stamps: If you have a few extra minutes at the Antigua airport, stop at the post office near the bank window and browse through the beautiful Antigua-Barbuda postage stamps. They are printed in deliciously bright colors with pictures of fruits, flowers, and wildlife.

WHERE TO STAY

Sunset View Resort
Belle Village, Barbuda, West Indies
Telephone: (809) 460-0435; fax: (809) 460-0266
Located about one-quarter mile outside Codrington near the Lagoon, this 11-room, two-story hotel is the most comfortable, reasonably priced accommodation on the island. Its simple and cozily modern rooms are neatly appointed. Especially attractive are the outdoor dining room and bar, in a garden setting with a swimming pool surrounded by goat-mown fields. Rates are $50 single or double. "We treat our guests like family," writes the new manager.

Coco Point Lodge
Box 90
St. John's, Antigua, West Indies
U.S. telephone: (212) 986-1416
Although Barbuda would not seem a likely setting for a luxury hotel, William Cody Kelly has succeeded in establishing a stunning, country club-like resort on the southern coast of the island. Single-level cottages and bungalows are situated on their own secluded sections of one of the Carib-

bean's most beautiful palm-lined beaches. The grounds and gardens are immaculately groomed, and the main house dining room and cocktail terrace face a breathtaking expanse of sand and sea. Vacations here are expensive barefoot escapes. The all-inclusive rates, which range from $250 to $600 per day, provide for all food, drinks, the use of tennis courts, boats, snorkeling equipment, and excursions.

Nedd's Guest House
Codrington, Barbuda, West Indies
Telephone: (809) 460-0059
Mr. McArthur Nedd has three clean and airy rooms upstairs above his minimart that go for $35 single and $50 double.

Guest Houses
The traveler on a more restricted budget will be able to find very basic accommodations in one of Codrington's several guest houses, including the Thomas House (which sells specially made postcards), located right next to the airport, and The Earl's, offering apartments and cottages in or near town. Detailed information is available from the Antigua-Barbuda Tourist Board, 610 Fifth Ave., Suite 311, New York, N.Y. 10020. Telephone: (212) 541-4117.

RESTAURANTS

Most visitors to Barbuda eat at their hotels or guest houses, but Jam City and the Lagoon Café at the jetty are popular with locals. Chez Blanche offers fine seafood dining at the Sunset View Resort.

HOW TO GET THERE

LIAT operates regularly scheduled morning and afternoon flights from Antigua to Barbuda.

PRACTICAL TIPS

Immigration: U.S. and Canadian citizens need only proof of identity. A passport is best, but a birth certificate (an original, not a photocopy) or a voter registration card will do. There is an $8 departure tax. A return or onward transportation ticket is required.

Currency: Barbuda uses the Eastern Caribbean dollar (EC), with an exchange rate of approximately 2.50 EC to U.S.$1. There is a bank at the Antigua airport where you can exchange your money before flying on to Barbuda.

Language: The official language is British English.

Montserrat

The natural beauty of Montserrat is abundantly evident as you fly in toward Blackburne Airport. The mountainous terrain is densely covered with dark green tropical foliage and forests. Misty clouds linger on the highest peaks. And the beauty only grows more intense as you get closer.

The warm hospitality of Montserrat is also abundantly evident as soon as you set foot in the tiny airport. The immigration officer asks where you are staying and offers his recommendations for lodging and car rentals. He will register you for a temporary driver's license after you have cleared customs. (It is best, however, to make your hotel decision on your own, after considering the options.) In the next room, the customs inspector hardly looks at your luggage; he is more interested in welcoming you to Montserrat. When he asks about the nature and extent of your visit, it seems less for official reasons than out of formal courtesy. And everything is accompanied by a smile.

Magnificent natural wonders and relaxed, informal hospitality are the key attractions of Montserrat, a 39-square-mile island 15 minutes by air from Antigua. It is an island of wonderful contrasts. Named by Christopher Columbus when he sailed by in 1493, Montserrat was first settled by Irish colonists (with a sprinkling of Scots and English) more than 350 years ago. The Irish influence is reflected in Montserrat's appropriate title as the "Emerald Island"; in such place-names as St. Patricks, Brodericks, Joe Morgan Hill, and Galway Plantation; and in the shamrock that is stamped onto your passport. But the modern population of 13,000 is mostly English-speaking and black. The island has been visited by pop music superstars because of its world-famous recording studio, yet it remains remarkably off the beaten track for most Caribbean tourists. It has a beautiful 100-acre golf course that seems anomalous amidst the vast expanses of lush unspoiled scenery. It is large enough to require auto transportation along its 115 miles of paved roads, but is best explored by foot from points where the roads end.

Plymouth is the main settlement, a partially rustic, partially modern village of 3,000 located on the sheltered west coast of Montserrat. The drive from Blackburne Airport, on the east side, takes you along winding roads, through fertile farmland, past hundreds of grazing goats and cattle, up through the hills dotted with private homes, and back down to the Caribbean shore. In town, the narrow avenues are a maze of one-way streets, running past centuries-old buildings, churches, and less interesting contemporary structures. Most visitors stay in or near Plymouth, taking advantage of the restaurants, car rentals, and easy access to the taxis that can carry you to the important sites north and south of town. During the day the streets are busy, with people gathering in conversation on the corners. But at night the town is still and looks virtually empty, especially in the summer season, with activity confined to the restaurants and pubs.

Although a hiker's paradise, with rewarding climbs and fascinating trails beckoning from all over the island, Montserrat cannot claim to be one of the Caribbean's best

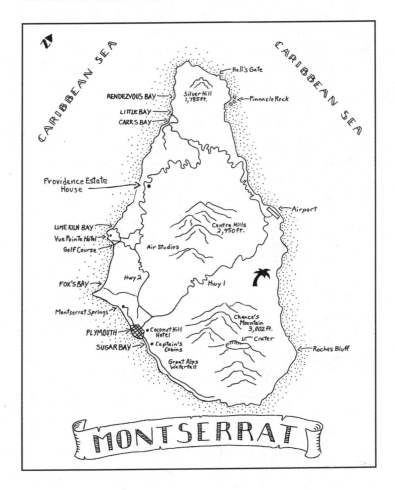

beach and diving locales. The waters are unpredictable, the coral reefs and coves few, and many of the beaches are gray and pebbly. But the Caribbean side of the island has the gentlest and warmest water, with good snorkeling at the best white sand beach near the Vue Pointe Hotel, and at Rendezvous and Carr's Bay. Interesting dives can be found at The Pinnacle, off Woodlands Bay; and the Artificial Reef, where the government once tried to attract sea life by dumping more than 200 old cars into 80 feet of water near Fones Bay. Windsurfing is available at the Vue Pointe Hotel.

But here, in contrast to such beach-bound heavens as Barbuda and the Bahamas, the water is almost an adjunct to the land. The possibilities for exploring the island are virtually limitless, from the exhilarating views from Old Fort on St. George's Hill, to the challenging climb up to the 3,000-foot peak of Mount Chance. Most people return to Montserrat year after year, knowing that they can feel welcomed and immediately at home, yet always finding something new to discover in the island's unique geographic splendor.

NOTEWORTHY

Great Alps Waterfall: We found a shortcut that knocked at least half an hour off the hiking time to this spectacular 70-foot waterfall, but we couldn't find our junction on the way back, and thus added at least another 30 minutes to the walk to our car. So it is recommended that you either hire a guide or start from the main entrance near the southern end of the island. The walk is long and humid, but well worth the exertion. As you approach the falls, the ferns and

Photo by Derk Richardson

Sunset from Rendezvous Bay

other broad-leafed plants grow to enormous heights. They add to the spiritual feeling that mounts as you finally reach the waterfall, which cascades down a sheer cliff into a small, slightly sulfurous pool. Take your time getting there and consider carrying water and a picnic lunch or snack.

Galway's Plantation: About a 15- or 20-minute drive south of Plymouth and up a winding ravine, the ruins of this 17th-century sugar plantation are being meticulously excavated. A windmill, sugar boiling house, and great house are available for investigation. And the view that ambitious Irish plantation owner David Galway commanded nearly 300 years ago has hardly changed.

Galway Soufriere is the bubbling, sulfurous center of a volcano in the southern section of Montserrat, just up the hill from Galway's plantation estate. A fascinating 20-minute walk from the road's end takes you along rugged volcanic rock to the steaming sulfur vents.

Fox's Bay Bird Sanctuary is located on the coast just north of Plymouth at Richmond Estate. Established as part of the Montserrat National Trust in 1979, it is the nesting place of egrets, herons, cuckoos, kingfishers, coots, and other species.

Stamps: Although you might start off looking for stamps at the Plymouth Post Office, be sure someone directs you to the Philatelic Building, where you can spend hours perusing the marvelous stamps at the Montserrat Stamp Shop. The natural wonders of the island, from lizards and fish to the towering peaks, are depicted in vivid color. They are among the most beautiful and sought-after stamps in the Caribbean.

The Montserrat Historical Society Museum, located in

an old sugar mill near Richmond Hill, houses exhibits reflecting the natural and cultural history of the island, as well as a fascinating postage stamp collection.

WHERE TO STAY

Vue Pointe Hotel
P.O. Box 65
Plymouth, Montserrat, West Indies
Telephone: (809) 491-5210; fax: (809) 491-48134; U.S. telephone: (800) 235-0709
The Vue Pointe has a widespread reputation as Montserrat's finest and friendliest hotel, to which many guests return year after year. But it is also the most expensive. Its 12 rooms and 28 hexagonal cottages are scattered among palm trees on spacious, neatly groomed grounds. Located next to Montserrat's beautiful Belham Valley Golf Course, it has a swimming pool with a spectacular sea view and is only about 100 yards from one of the island's best beaches. The special Wednesday night barbecue, with live steel band music, is a popular event. Rates start at $90 in summer (April 14-December 15) and $126 in winter. Cottages range from $126 in low season, to $166 in high.

Montserrat Springs Hotel
Box 259
Plymouth, Montserrat, West Indies
Telephone: (809) 491-2481; fax: (809) 491-4070
There are 17 garden rooms and six efficiency suites with kitchen at this pleasant small resort overlooking Emerald Isle Beach. Guests enjoy use of a swimming pool and two

tennis courts. Winter rates range from $145 for a double to $175 for a suite.

Providence Estate House

St. Peter's, Montserrat, West Indies

Telephone: (809) 491-6476; fax: (809) 491-8476

Located on a hilltop overlooking the sea, this bed and breakfast inn has two poolside guest rooms with private bath, kitchenette, and cable TV. Rates in this historical restored house surrounded by gardens range from $70 to $85 for two.

Niggy's Guest House

Aymers Ghaut

Kinsale, Montserrat, West Indies

Telephone (809) 491-7489

This small and friendly five-room guest house is a good choice for budget travelers. Breakfast, lunch and dinner are served in the hospitable dining room. Rates year-round are $20 double and $15 single.

Apartments and Villa Rentals

Many visitors to Montserrat rent a house or an apartment. There are many choices in Plymouth and around the island. For weekly or monthly rentals contact the Montserrat Tourist Board, P.O. Box 7, Plymouth, Montserrat, W.I. Telephone: (809) 491-2230; fax: (809) 491-7430.

RESTAURANTS

The Attic is popular for its homey cuisine and breezy rooftop dining with a superb view.

Mole's Bar is a favorite local meeting place for breakfast, lunch, and drinks.

Belham Valley in Plymouth is the choice for an elegant meal in a romantic setting.

FROM MY JOURNAL

We rented a car in Plymouth today and learned how to drive on the left side of the road with the steering wheel on the right—first through the narrow one-way streets of town, then on the thin winding road to the southern end of the island. Drivers here know every curve and bump; there's no time to be nervous. Away from town, the task is easier, but it's a relief to park the car and walk off into the jungle. I'd just as soon throw the keys into the sea and stay on foot. The morning drive back over the mountain to the airport is spectacular. Mists rise from the ground dampened overnight by sudden rain showers, and the sun streams through the leftover clouds. I'm ready to toss my plane ticket into the sea, as well.

HOW TO GET THERE

LIAT and Montserrat Airways have regularly scheduled flights from Antigua to Blackburne Airport on the northeast coast of Montserrat. Winair provides daily flights from St. Martin.

PRACTICAL TIPS

Immigration: A valid passport or proof of identity is required for entry, plus a return or onward transportation ticket. The departure tax is $10.

Currency: The currency on Montserrat is the Eastern Caribbean dollar (EC), with an exchange rate of approximately 2.70 EC to U.S.$1.

Language: It's English with a brogue, a result of the Irish legacy.

Photo courtesy of Montserrat Tourist Board

The 75-foot Great Alps Waterfall

FRENCH WEST INDIES

A beach on Marie-Galante Island

Marie-Galante

It is an enigma that an island as large as Marie-Galante, with such superb beaches and quiet country roads, can be so undiscovered. Rarely will you find more than a handful of visitors from anywhere beyond Guadeloupe. Even at Christmas, while other islands are packed to capacity, the beaches on Marie-Galante are relatively empty. The only possible explanation is that barely a word of English is spoken anywhere on the island, and most of the local inhabitants have a very "laissez-faire" attitude about visitors. For the intrepid traveler who does not mind the challenge of a French-speaking island not geared to tourism, the rewards are many.

The trip from Pointe-à-Pitre, Guadeloupe, is an easy one, either by ferry (one hour) or by air (15 minutes, landing on the flat plain a few miles south of Grand-Bourg). Coming immediately into view are the sugarcane fields and idle 19th-century stone windmills. Grand-Bourg, a town of 10,000 inhabitants, is a busy scene of ugly concrete structures mixed with more interesting wooden buildings. The balconies over the sidewalks are similar to those in the

Latin Quarter of New Orleans, and there is a covered outdoor market where colorfully-dressed women sell spices, fruit, vegetables, and clothing.

To explore the island beyond the principal town of Grand-Bourg (GAM-bo in patois), ten-passenger minibuses can be hailed like taxis from 6:00 a.m. to 5:00 p.m. You get off anywhere along the route and pay the 5F ($0.60) tariff as you exit. As you ride along the oceanfront road to the smaller towns of St. Louis and Capesterre, there is the temptation to stop, as each beach becomes progressively more inviting. Snorkeling at Capesterre is excellent, and from here it is a very long swim or a short walk to Les Galeries, massive and impressive rock formations that have been carved out by the surf. Continuing inland, Trou a Diable is a magnificent cave for the adventurous. It is some 550 yards long with an underground lake. Safer, perhaps, is the marvelous walk along the cliff-fringed coast, with its rocky promontories and secluded coves, to Caye Plate, a steep-sided crag with extensive views, where local fishermen catch crayfish of exceptional size.

Marie-Galante is a delight to explore. Each turn of the coast offers another marvelous vista, secluded cove, or immense stretch of quiet beach. Staying here is like returning to another era, before the tourism boom of the 1950s covered many islands with high-rise hotels and curio shops.

NOTEWORTHY

Habitation Murat is a baroque style plantation manor built in the 18th century and destroyed by earthquake in 1843. It is now a museum with sea life exhibits. The restored windmill is the most fascinating building on the estate grounds, and from the tower there are commanding views of Dominica.

Vieux-Fort, an Old World village on a fine beach, is a fascinating collection of pile dwellings, which were common all over the island until the 19th century.

Plage du Massacre is a fine, long beach with many excellent picnic spots beneath shady trees. This is a quieter, less populated part of the island.

Saint Louis, a town of 4,000 inhabitants, is worth exploring on foot. The old, weathered stores and houses on

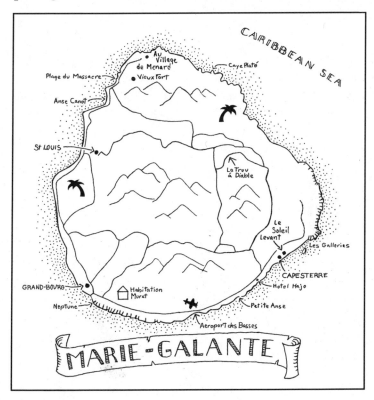

the back streets are infinitely more interesting than the new concrete of Capesterre and Grand-Bourg. Along the waterfront multicolored fishing boats glisten on the clear, calm sea in the bright sun. A fine beach is just minutes to the north by foot.

WHERE TO STAY

Hotel Hajo
Capesterre, Marie-Galante
97112 Guadeloupe, French West Indies
Telephone: (011) 590-97-32-76
Mediterranean in style, with unusual sculpture and furniture, each of the six rooms at Hajo faces the sea. Rarely will you see many guests, except during French holidays, when visitors come from Guadeloupe. Food is French and Creole, excellent and hearty, served on the seaside veranda. The location could not be better: it is a ten-minute walk to the village of Capesterre or a five-minute walk to one of the best beaches on the island. Rates start at $65 for two.

Le Soleil Levant
42, rue de la Marine
Capsterre, 97140 Marie-Galante
Guadeloupe, French West Indies
Located in the town of Capsterre, there are ten air-conditioned double bedrooms at 290 francs (includes continental breakfast) and two family apartments with kitchen at 400 and 500 francs each. On the grounds are a swimming pool and a big playgarden for children. The owner, Monsieur Bade, speaks a little English.

Au Village de Menard
97112 Grand-Bourg, Marie-Galante
Guadeloupe, French West Indies
Telephone: (011) 590-97-77-02; fax: (011) 590-97-76-89
Located on the northern tip of the island (but not on the sea), with a view towards Guadeloupe, the seven modern housekeeping bungalows are clean and comfortable. There is a small covered dining porch which faces the swimming pool. The nearest town for restaurants and shops is five miles away at Saint Louis. Christianne Le Maistre will be happy to mail you a color brochure in either English or French (the first color brochure we've seen on the island). Rates range from 300-500 francs.

RESTAURANTS

Tatie Zezette, Plage la Feuillere, Capesterre, offers very good Creole cuisine with vintage wine. The owner is charming, but you must speak French. Telephone: (011) 590-97-96-84.

Neptune, Rue Beaurenon ze Pont, Grand-Bourg, offers delicious pizza *jambon* and reasonable French seafood dishes, including *mousseline de poisson, langoustes, coquille d'oursins gratinées, darne de daurade au poivre vert*, and wood-grilled fish and meat. Telephone: (011) 590-97-96-90.

Chez Henri et Baptiste, in Saint Louis, is a very charming, intimate restaurant with excellent food. But here, as at all restaurants on Marie-Galante, you should give an hour's notice before you arrive, so they can turn on the generator and buy the food. Since there are literally no tourists, each restaurant will be your own private dining room. No telephone.

HOW TO GET THERE

There is a regular ferry service (one hour, $7) from Pointe-à-Pitre, Guadeloupe, to Grand-Bourg, Marie-Galante, and several daily flights on Air Guadeloupe (15 minutes, $35 one way). Reconfirm return air reservations on arrival.

Photo by Clayton Call

Local children at St. Louis Town Hall

Terre-de-Haut

One Caribbean island is so ideal that the visitor has to wonder why few people other than Jacques Cousteau have discovered it and made it their home. Its striking terrain; panoramic vistas; empty, breathtaking beaches and dazzling water; gracious population; and fine cuisine all conspire to make it a genuine paradise. If its dependence on rain for drinking water did not inhibit future development, I would be reluctant to even divulge the name of this, one of my favorite islands. Fortunately, Terre-de-Haut will remain relatively unspoiled, as it can sustain only a small number of visitors at any one time.

Isle des Saintes is a tiny cluster of islands seven miles off the southwestern tip of Guadeloupe. Terre-de-Haut (more often referred to as Les Saintes) is the archipelago's island metropolis, although it is less than six square miles in size and has fewer than 5,000 inhabitants. And it is the only island with several choices of accommodation.

The beaches on Les Saintes are marvelous; swimming and snorkeling are excellent. But that is only one small part of this island's appeal. Because the remarkable hilly terrain

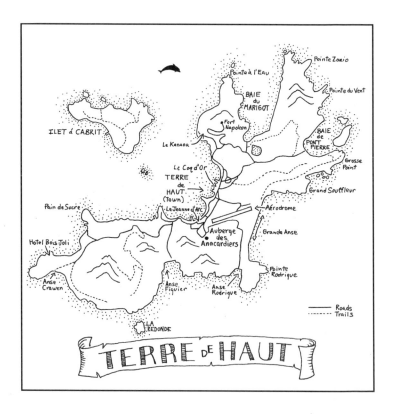

Pointe Zazio
Pointe à l'Eau
Pointe du Vent
BAIE du MARIGOT
Fort Napoleon
ILET à CABRIT
Le Kanaoa
BAIE de PONT PIERRE
Grosse Point
Le Coq d'Or
TERRE de HAUT. (Town)
Grand Souffleur
Pain de Sucre
Le Jeanne d'Arc
Aérodrome
Auberge des Anacardiers
Grande Anse
Hotel Bois Joli
Pointe Rodrique
Anse Crawen
Anse Figuier
Anse Rodrigue
Roads
Trails
LA REDONDE

TERRE DE HAUT

of Les Saintes is unsuited for agriculture, the French never colonized the islands for anything but strategic reasons. There was no plantation system and thus, no legacy of slave labor. The peaceful relationship between the French and the native Santois has resulted in a minimum of racial tension and economic disparity. Poverty, unemployment, and crime are unknown here; there isn't even a jail.

Of the mere dozen vehicles on the island, most are taxi vans used for airport transportation, for school outings to the beach, or occasionally, ambulances. The narrow concrete roads thus become extra wide "sidewalks," where you can stroll leisurely without the intrusion of motor traffic. One can easily walk anywhere on the island in less than an hour.

Terre-de-Haut is the island's major town. A picturesque little settlement of small, red-roofed houses, it is centrally located on a curving bay between the hills. These charming houses and stores are spotlessly clean and beautifully adorned with colorful vines and myriad flowers in dozens of pots and jars. This is not a town reconstructed for the sake of tourism; it is a neatly maintained fishing village where life revolves around the sea. Purple, pink, and mauve fishing nets are used to haul in the daily catch. What is not consumed in private homes behind 18th-century doors is sold to the local restaurants. Terre-de-Haut hosts frequent weekend visitors from Guadeloupe, who enjoy fine dining

Photo by Clayton Call

View of town harbor from Fort Napoleon

at the many small restaurants along the waterfront and back streets. The cuisine of Les Saintes is French and Creole, and consistently superb.

NOTEWORTHY

Pain du Sucre: The tiny, exquisitely beautiful double cove at Pain du Sucre is hard to find. In fact, I only discovered it on my second visit when some locals asked the taxi van to stop on my way back to Hotel Bois Joli. Carrying towels and snorkeling gear, they disappeared suddenly on the steep path beneath the road. Their destination was this marvelous hidden spot, where snorkeling is excellent. And should you become thirsty or hungry, there is even a small, informal beach restaurant. To get here from town, ask the taxi van

Excursion boat leaving town harbor

for Pain du Sucre, or take the Hotel Bois Joli boat and, for an extra few francs, ask them to stop. By foot, you can reach the cove through a hilly, 40-minute walk from town.

Pont-Pierre Beach: Totally protected by cliffs, this unspoiled, undeveloped bay is one of the most beautiful in the Caribbean. Visitors from Guadeloupe come on the weekends for the fine snorkeling and swimming, but even then it is hardly overcrowded. Limited camping is available for a nominal fee.

Fort Napoleon: Built at the beginning of the 19th century to replace an earlier 17th-century fort, Fort Napoleon contains a small museum. The 30-minute walk is pleasant, and the views make the climb worthwhile.

Morne du Chameau: At 1,014 feet, this is the highest point on the island. From the top you can enjoy breathtaking panoramic views of Guadeloupe to the north, Marie-Galante to the east, and Dominica to the south.

WHERE TO STAY

Hotel Bois Joli
Terre-de-Haut, 97137 Les Saintes
via Guadeloupe, French West Indies
Telephone: (011) 590-99-50-38, fax: (011) 590-99-55-05
This hotel has a very private location, along the coast one mile from town. The rooms in the old main building are small and simple, but have wonderful views, especially on the second floor. The newer wing is directly on the water, a short walk from the main building and beyond the new swimming pool. Swimming is excellent, and the snorkeling is good at the far end of the beach near the rocks. You can

walk or ride the taxi van to town, but the more serene choice is by sea. The local ferry makes this short, scenic trip several times per day. But for freedom and flexibility, you can't beat renting your own boat. Rates at Bois Joli start at $160 for two, but this includes two meals a day.

Jeanne d'Arc

Terre-de-Haut, 97137 Les Saintes
via Guadeloupe, French West Indies
Telephone: (011) 590-99-50-41
This small, ten-room beachfront hotel is situated at the end of the village, within walking distance of the town's plaza, wharf, and restaurants. The best rooms face the beach and rent for approximately $50 per night.

Les Petits Saints aux Anacardiers

(also called Auberge des Anacardiers)
Terre-de-Haut, 97137 Les Saintes
via Guadeloupe, French West Indies
Telephone: (011) 590-99-50-99; fax: (011) 590-99-54-51
You can be assured a warm welcome at this newest addition to the island's accommodations. Owner Didier Spindler, a painter and antique collector, designed and furnished this charming "auberge" built around a swimming pool on a hillside overlooking the harbor. The best rooms face the sea; the hillside rooms can be dark and airless. Not all rooms have private baths. The shared showers and toilets are spotlessly clean, but most American visitors will find them "diminutively chic." Secluded and quiet, Anacardiers is just a very short walk to the beach or town. Breakfast and a superb dinner are included in the daily rate of $140 for two.

Le Village Creole

Terre-de-Haut, 97137 Iles des Saintes
Guadeloupe, French West Indies
Telephone: (011) 590-99-53-83
There are fully equipped kitchens at this charming one-
and two-bedroom unit complex, located in a quiet waterfront location a short walk to town. Daily rates per couple
start at $130 in summer, and $150 in winter.

Le Kanaoa

Terre-de-Haut, 97137 Les Saintes
via Guadeloupe, French West Indies
Telephone: (011) 590-99-51-36; fax: (011) 590-99-55-04
This lively waterfront hotel and restaurant has 19 charming
rooms—many with balconies overlooking the bay—and a
swimming pool.

APARTMENTS/HOUSE RENTALS

There are now at least a dozen studio and house rentals on
Terre-de-Haut. "Ti Santois," a pocket guide to the island, lists
phone numbers for each of the rentals. You can get a complimentary copy from the Guadeloupe Tourist Board, B.P.
1099; 5 Square de la Banque; 97181 Point-à-Pitre, Guadeloupe, French West Indies. Telephone: (011) 590-82-09-03;
fax (011) 590-83-89-22.

CAMPING

Camping is allowed at Pont-Pierre Beach, one of the most
beautiful undeveloped bays in the Caribbean.

RESTAURANTS

It is probably impossible to get a bad meal from any of the dozen or so small restaurants on Les Saintes. Among the local delicacies are *crabes farçis*, stuffed crab; *accra*, a small fritter of cod or malanga root; *daube de lambis*, a conch stew; *blaff*, made with fish or sea urchins; *ragoût de chartrous*, small octopus served with red beans; and *poulet à la noix de coco*, local free-range chicken cooked in coconut milk. Desserts include bananas *flambés* and the Les Saintes' specialty, *tourment d'amour* (coconut tarts), often sold on the streets by the island's beautiful children.

FROM MY JOURNAL

Carnival on Terre-de-Haut last night was a festival of color, music, and a small island's friendly *joie de vivre*. Young and old danced together en masse in the town plaza by the wharf. Many beautiful painted faces were crowned with thick blond hair, Sweden's legacy to these fair islands. Next time, we'll definitely want to participate with costumes.

HOW TO GET THERE

Air Guadeloupe has daily 15-minute flights from Pointe-à-Pitre, Guadeloupe to Terre-de-Haut. By sea, regular ferry service is offered from Trois-Rivieres on Guadeloupe (8:30 a.m. Monday through Saturday, 7:30 a.m. on Sunday). From Pointe-à-Pitre, the ferry leaves daily at 8:00 a.m. and returns at 4:00 p.m. Contact Trans-Antilles Express for schedules. Telephone: (011) 590-82-12-45.

Terre-de-Bas

The other inhabited island of Les Saintes, Terre-de-Bas, is only three miles from Terre-de-Haut, but is remarkably separate. Now, however, there is regular boat service several times a day from the Terre-de-Haut wharf. Overnight lodging is available, and for the intrepid traveler, Terre-de-Bas is well worth exploring. A walker's paradise, criss-crossed with scenic hiking trails and small one-lane roads, the island can be explored at the leisurely pace found only in such undiscovered spots.

The road begins at the ferry landing at Anse des Muriers. Just a few hundred yards inland, at the first fork in the road, you encounter Arlette's Restaurant, a source of good food and valuable information about the island. The small road to the left leads to Grand Anse, a tiny village clustered around a primitive 17th-century church. Swimmers and snorkelers will want to take this detour to Grand Anse and enjoy refreshing drinks at the beachside "lolos."

Back on the main cross-island road past Arlette's, each bend offers a different and more spectacular view before the final descent into Petites Anses. Island life is focused here around the town hall, post office, fire station, dispensary, school, church, cemetery, hotel, and restaurant. Next to the marina, colorful "Santois" fishing boats line the beach, and fishing nets dry in the warm sun.

WHERE TO STAY

Au Poisson-Volant
Petites Anses, Terre-de-Bas
97137 Iles des Saintes
via Guadeloupe, French West Indies
Telephone: (011) 590-99-80-47
The only hotel in town has nine spartan rooms with questionable plumbing and very little water pressure, but the local Santois woman is so hospitable, and the delicious

Photo by Burl Willes

View of Terre-de-Bas from Terre-de-Haut

Creole food so good, that any noise or inconvenience is soon forgotten. You may share the dining room with a happy group of French day-trippers, but at night you'll rarely see another visitor. There is a small beach 15 minutes downhill from the hotel, a great place to watch the sunset. Rates are approximately $50 per night, per room.

It is possible to rent a room with meals at Chez Renaud Vala or Chez Arlette. Telephone: (011) 590-99-81-66. A knowledge of French is almost essential on Terre-de-Bas, unless you are confident that you can get by with mime and sign language.

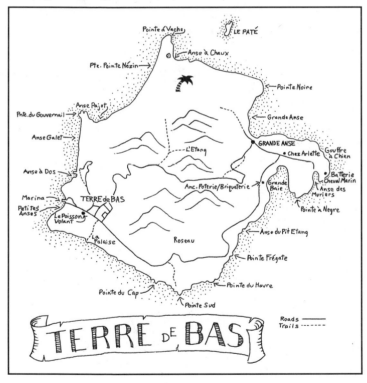

HOW TO GET THERE

There is now regular ferry service five or six times a day from the Terre-de-Haut wharf; it stops briefly at the Hotel Bois Joli en route. The crossing time is approximately 30 minutes, and the fare is $12 round trip. Reservations are not taken, unless you plan a day excursion, which will include lunch at the Poisson-Volant.

PRACTICAL TIPS

Since there are few hotels on Les Saintes, it is important to have a reservation in the peak seasons: December 15-March 15, Bastille Day (July 14), and Liberation Day (August 15-17).

Take a flashlight, as the roads are not lit at night, and on moonless nights the countryside beyond town is pitch dark.

Immigration: An onward or return ticket and a valid passport are required.

Currency: The official currency is the French franc, which fluctuates between 4F to 6F to U.S.$1.

Language: French is the official language, but English is spoken in some hotels and restaurants.

GRENADINES

The Grenadine Islands are simply sensational. There are more than 120 of them in the 50 miles between St. Vincent and Grenada, but only 11 are inhabited. They are a boat owner's paradise: very tropical, hilly islands with many fine harbors and coves, constant breezes, charming villages, friendly people, and superb, uncrowded beaches. The most beautiful and undiscovered of the inhabited islands are now accessible to anyone willing to make the effort to get there. Several of the islands have small airports, and there is local boat service to the others.

Starting at the top in the St. Vincent Grenadines, Bequia is a well-discovered international destination. It is a beautiful island with many fine small hotels and excellent beaches. Loyal visitors return year after year to this friendly island, accessible only by boat from St. Vincent. Mustique has marvelous beaches and coves, and an international crowd is attracted to the Cotton House Hotel and the island's 50 private houses, which give this pleasant place its celebrity status. To the south, Canouan never has more than two dozen visitors at any one time; there are just two small beachfront hotels, a handful of cars, and 600 hospitable people. Not far away, Mayreau is a return to another century, so undiscovered that no one on Carriacou (ten miles away) knew if there were any inhabitants or any place to spend the night! Spectacular Union Island, with two lofty peaks rising from the aquamarine sea, has its share of yachts, but still remains quiet and friendly. Here also are Petit St. Vincent, Palm Island, and Young Island, the three privately owned and fairly well-publicized resort islands of the Grenadines. Crossing the border from the St. Vincent Grenadines to the Grenada Grenadines, Petit Martinique and Carriacou bring the total number to five exceptional, undiscovered jewels in the Grenadine crown: Canouan, Mayreau, Union, Petit Martinique, and Carriacou.

Carriacou

Carriacou's 13 square miles of towering hills and white sand beaches make it the largest and most populated of the Grenadines. It is also one of the most beautiful and certainly the most interesting. On this rich agricultural island, the Scots settled in Windward, the French in L'Esterre, and the English in Hillsborough, leaving an influence still in evidence today. This European heritage mixes with descendants of black slaves, who have preserved many old cultural and spiritual traditions resembling the Xango of Trinidad and the voodoo cult of Haiti.

In the town of Windward, villagers of Scottish descent carry on the tradition of building wooden schooners from local white cedar. Skeletons of boats in various stages of completion are often seen on the beach, where workers use centuries-old techniques and rudimentary tools to create the West Indian trade schooner fleet. Many of the Windward boats sail in the Carriacou Regatta, held during the first weekend in August. It is a wonderful time to visit, as the island's 8,000 inhabitants celebrate on land as well as on sea.

The sounds of conga drums fill the air, and all eyes turn toward the dancers, who celebrate the harvest of the land and sea with dances handed down over generations. The people of Carriacou remember the African tribes from which they came—Congo, Moko, Mandinka, Ibo, Kromanti—and their dances are sensational. The island's four-day festivities also include swimming, sailing model boats, and playing ball games, tug-of-war, and everyone's favorite, greasy pole.

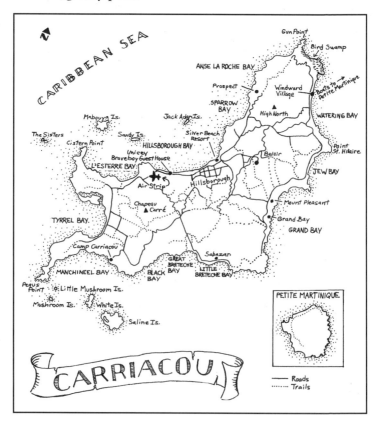

Photo by Clayton Call

Hillsborough Market

By the Wednesday after the festival, the Hillsborough town has returned to its normal level of activity. With a population of just under 900, there are few traffic jams, no stop lights, and no need to hurry. Main Street parallels the beach. Built of stone and shingle, many of the stores have fascinating names: the Industrious Store, the Family Store (a good place to buy stamps), Morning Star Bakery, No Trust, Trust Is to Burst, and No Hell. Near the pier is the post office, the fruit and vegetable market, and the government customs office.

Leaving the town and heading north into the hills toward Windward, the nature lover will delight in the flora and fauna of this lush, tropical island. Bougainvillea and flamboyants flourish, and there are many varieties of cactus. Sugar apples, papayas, and limes are abundant. The dogwood and white immortelle are two Carriacou trees unknown in Grenada. The southern mockingbird, the Antillean grackle, and the yellow bananaquit are the most common birds (the yellow bananaquit is rare in Grenada). Among others to be seen are glossy cowbirds, ramiers, ground doves, wood doves, kingbirds, elaenias, emerald-throated hummingbirds, and frigate birds. Not often seen but occasionally heard is the mangrove cuckoo.

NOTEWORTHY

Sandy Island, just off Carriacou, is a wonderful place for snorkeling and picnicking. Other nearby islets are the Sisters, Mabouya, and Jack-A-Dan.

Carriacou Museum, on a side street off Main in Hillsborough, has an interesting collection of Amerindian and European artifacts. Small and friendly, this little museum is a rarity for such a small island.

Tyrrel Bay, on the west side, is a spectacular enclosed bay, where the water is always calm and serene. Paradise Beach is a favorite for locals, and the swimming here is excellent.

WHERE TO STAY

Silver Beach Resort
Carriacou, Grenada, West Indies
Telephone: (809) 443-7337; fax: (809) 443-7165
Local islanders, the Bullen family, own and manage this small, friendly resort located on the water's edge a short walk from town. There are four duplex cottages, each with a kitchen and patio facing the garden, and ten ocean view suites with balconies overlooking the bay. There is a scuba-diving base, and swimming and snorkeling in front of the hotel are excellent. The house bus offers daily siteseeing tours and complimentary transfers to and from the airport on request. Fresh local seafood (including conch and lobster) and a variety of West Indian dishes are featured in the restaurant. Rates start at $80 in summer, $112 in winter.

The Caribbee Inn
Prospect
Carriacou, Grenada, West Indies
Telephone: (809) 443-7380; fax: (809) 443-8142
At the end of a long, potholed dirt road on a hill 200 yards above the sea, and bordering the edge of a proposed national park, Caribbee Inn is restful and quiet. English

owners and managers Robert and Wendy Cooper offer comfortable, spacious suites with traditional four-poster beds, outstanding food, a library, snorkel gear, helpful advice, and a local boatman for excursions to other islands. The Planter's Suite, a self-contained unit with bedroom, kitchen, bath, and private porch, has the best view. The Villa, in a separate building, has two bedrooms, kitchen, and bath. Meandering pathways lead down through six acres of private grounds to a secluded cove. Rates start at $90 double in summer, $120 in winter. Breakfast and dinner (perhaps the best food on the island) are $35 per person extra.

Unicey Braveboy
Lauriston
Carriacou, Grenada, West Indies
Telephone: (809) 443-7471
For the traveler on a budget, Unicey Braveboy runs a guest house in Lauriston, facing the quiet road and beach. There is a communal bathroom and kitchen, and rates begin at $25 per day.

Private Villa and Cottage Rentals
Down Island, Ltd.
Carriacou, Grenada, West Indies
Telephone and fax: (809) 443-8182
Note: When writing for reservations, keep in mind that mail can take two weeks in each direction.

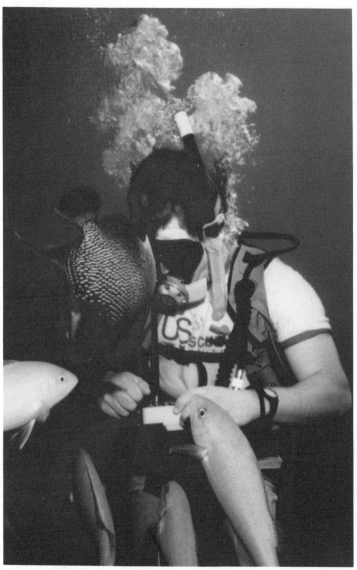

A diver explores some of Carriacou's varied marine life

RESTAURANTS

Tip Top Restaurant and Bar, on Main Street, is known for its good local dishes.

Roof Gardens Restaurant and Bar, facing the jetty and market, features seafood and local foods. Cassada Bay offers West Indian cuisine, specializing in lobster, oysters, conch, and fish.

The Italian Restaurant, on a hill overlooking Tyrrel Bay, is quaint and homey and serves fine Italian food.

Try the fresh currant or coconut rolls at Gramma's Bakery.

Non-residents are welcome at the Caribbee Inn, where the food is fresh, local, and French-Creole inspired.

Hillsborough Bar serves good food without a reservation.

HOW TO GET THERE

There is now direct air service on American Airlines from the U.S. to Grenada. B.W.I.A. International has direct service from New York and Miami to Barbados. LIAT flies from Barbados and Grenada, and interisland boats travel from St. Vincent and Grenada. Sailing time is three hours from Grenada or 20 minutes by plane.

Petit Martinique

The extinct volcanic peak of Petit Martinique rises dramatically from the sea, a beckoning Bali Hai to those on nearby Carriacou. From the village of Windward, it is easy to arrange a boat for the 30-minute, three-mile trip across varying shades of blue water to the reef-protected island.

Veralyn "Ann" Jones, a beautiful and intelligent lady from New York, joined me on the boat trip to Petit Martinique. For her, this first visit was extremely special. Her father, John Jones, was born on this quiet island of 600 industrious black inhabitants. On arrival the beach was a hub of boating activity—painting, polishing, and other last-minute preparations for the annual regatta. There are no paved roads and no cars on the island, so it was easy to explore this charming, quiet island by foot.

NOTEWORTHY

The hike to the top of Petit Martinique's highest peak affords a spectacular view of the surrounding islands: Petit St. Vincent, Carriacou, Union, Canouan, and several uninhabited islands.

Photo by Burl Willes

Petit Martinique from Windward Village

WHERE TO STAY

Mrs. Petroilla Ceasar

Petit Martinique via Carriacou, Grenada, West Indies

The only rooms and food on the island are available at this tiny, friendly gathering place.

Union Island

The flight from Carriacou to Union Island takes just five minutes, barely time to marvel at the islands below: Petit Martinique, Petit St. Vincent, and Palm Island. The landing over the harbor town of Clifton, with white sailboats shining on the glimmering azure sea, is spectacular; it passes so quickly that you long for a slow-motion rerun.

The picturesque airport building is an international arrival point to the St. Vincent Grenadines, but rarely do more than two or three passengers enter here from neighboring Carriacou in the Grenada Grenadines. The immigration officer is delighted to see a new arrival to his island, and with passport shown and duly stamped, the visitor is free to leave. The unusual, mountainous beauty of Union is immediately overwhelming.

The plane has departed for Mustique, and the stillness of the island adds to the allure of its tropical remoteness. On one side Mount Taboi rises to 1,000 feet; and on the other is the sea. Here on Union there is no traffic, there are no screeching motorbikes, no buses, no taxis. A grassy path lined with conch shells shows the way across the runway to the Anchorage Hotel. From there along the waterfront and beach, it is a five-minute walk to Clifton town, comprised of several general stores, markets, a minuscule tourist office, two small, locally owned hotels, a few bars and restaurants, and shops selling local handicrafts.

Union Island is a hiker's paradise. The walks are many, and all are rewarding. Crossing the island to the north are Richmond Bay and Belmont Bay. The English-speaking inhabitants along the way are friendly, as are the ubiquitous, well-behaved brown goats.

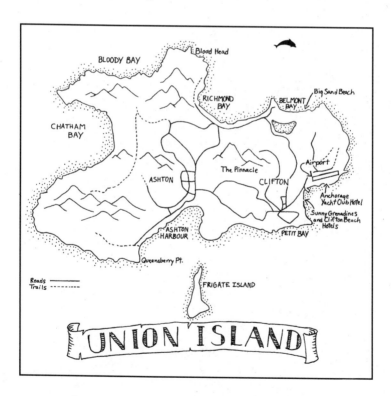

NOTEWORTHY

Chatham Bay is a beautiful and sequestered bay on the east coast, with excellent swimming. Frigate Island, part of the Lagoon Reef that protects almost the entire south coast, is an ideal place for snorkeling.

WHERE TO STAY

Anchorage Yacht Club
Clifton
Union Island, St. Vincent Grenadines
Telephone: (809) 458-8221; fax: (809) 458-8365
The ten cabanas and bungalows in a coconut grove facing the sea are very comfortable, and there are an additional five rooms upstairs in the main building overlooking the outdoor restaurant. This is a French-managed hotel, popular with international yachters who often anchor offshore and enjoy the space of a cabana or bungalow for a few days of elbow room and hot showers. Scuba lessons and equipment are available. Double rooms start at $90, and bungalows at $140.

Sunny Grenadines Hotel
Clifton
Union Island, St. Vincent Grenadines
Telephone: (809) 458-8327
King Mitchell, a retired Union Island seaman, welcomes travelers to his informal waterfront hotel set in a quiet garden. The duplex units facing the sea are the ones to request. Mr. Mitchell is happy to arrange inexpensive boat

trips to Tobago Cays (excellent snorkeling) and neighboring islands. Rates start at $50 single, and $65 for two.

Clifton Beach Hotel
Clifton
Union Island, St. Vincent Grenadines
Telephone: (809) 458-8235
There are ten rooms with private baths facing the beach of Clifton town harbor. The rooms are spartan but comfortable, and the staff is friendly. Clifton Beach Hotel is also owned by a local islander, Conrad Adams. Rates start at $50 single and $65 double.

Approaching Union Island on the inter-island ferry

Travelers on a tight budget will be warmly welcomed at the Clifton Beach Guest House in Clifton town.

RESTAURANTS

The only food on Union Island is served at your guest house or hotel.

HOW TO GET THERE

There is air service on LIAT from Barbados, St. Vincent, Grenada, and Carriacou and on Air Martinique to points north—St. Vincent, Dominica, and Martinique. The local boat from St. Vincent leaves at 10:00 a.m. on Monday and Thursday and returns on Tuesday and Friday, but do reconfirm sailing schedule with your hotel or guest house.

Mayreau

The centuries dissolve as the interisland ferry disappears around a distant point, and the visitor is alone to discover the tranquil beauty of the island. Mayreau (population 100) is small—only 1½ square miles—yet on foot, it seems much larger. There are no roads and no cars. There are goats, sheep, virgin beaches, the land, and the sea. The vistas are exceptional, and from the church above the village there is a spectacular panorama of Canouan, Union, Tobago Cays, Petit St. Vincent, and Grenada.

Life on Mayreau revolves around the sea, fishing, and sailing. The wooden houses are small, but not without character, and many have small subsistence vegetable gardens. A true sense of community pervades the island. Everyone meets for mass in the charming stone Catholic church, with its magnificent view. In this very quiet, rural island existence, no one goes without if help is needed. Rarely will you see another person on the beaches—except perhaps a fisherman or occasionally, a visiting yachtsman who has anchored in Salt Whistle Bay. To stay overnight or for a few days offers an experience rarely felt in the 20th century.

NOTEWORTHY

The walk across the island's lowland to the windward side is worth taking. In the dry season there are intricate crystals of rock salt in an original salt pond, and on the beach there are shells and interesting driftwood.

The Tobago Cays (excellent snorkeling) are just 30 minutes away by sailboat.

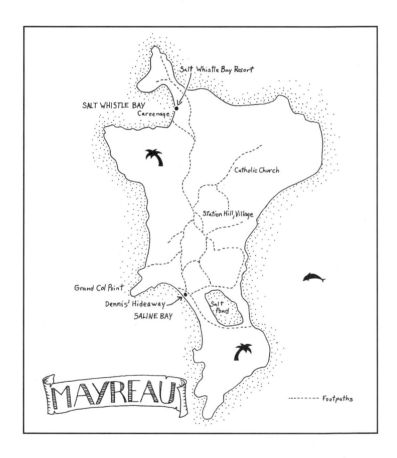

WHERE TO STAY

Salt Whistle Bay Club

Mayreau via Union Island, St. Vincent Grenadines

Telephone: (809) 458-8444

German/Canadian owners Undine and Tom Potter have created a unique, relaxed and non-intrusive "resort" on an idyllic beach. The island's stone bungalows are decorated with rattan furnishings and batiks, with hammocks on the roof decks. Rates start at $250 in low season, and include breakfast and dinner.

Dennis' Hideaway

Mayreau via Union Island, St. Vincent Grenadines

Telephone and fax: (809) 458-8594

Owner Dennis Forde, a former charter yacht captain born on Mayreau, started a small bar and restaurant eight years ago. Now there is a house with two twin-bedded rooms and a shared bath. The public sitting room has a television, video, stereo and many books. The view of Saline Bay from the balcony is truly wonderful. Their *Mayreau Queen*, a 39-foot sailing yacht, is available for day charters to neighboring Tobago Cays, Palm Island, and Petit St. Vincent. Snorkeling and fishing equipment are provided. Rates in the guest house are $25 per person, low season, and $35 in high season.

RESTAURANTS

Dennis' Hideaway restaurant in Mayreau Village, Saline Bay, serves excellent grilled fish, lobster, shrimp, and conch on the pleasant garden terrace.

HOW TO GET THERE

The interisland ferry will make a stop at Mayreau when requested to do so. The Salt Whistle Bay Club will meet guests by private launch at nearby Union Island.

Photo by Burl Willes

A Mayreau beach

Canouan

Waiting for the small launch to arrive for the move from schooner to shore, one can tell even before setting foot on Canouan that it is a beach lover's paradise. On this quiet island, the beaches are long, empty, and incredibly white against the calm turquoise sea.

On shore the island is brown and rather barren in the lowland, yet very green and tropical in the hills. The jungle casts its shadow on the end of Grand Bay and turns the water an emerald green, for a never-to-be-forgotten swim at sunset.

Fishing, farming, and sailing occupy most of the island's 700 shy but friendly English-speaking inhabitants. The roads are not paved, and only very occasionally will you need to step aside for a passing jeep.

NOTEWORTHY

On the island's east side there are many excellent deserted beaches and coves that are easy to reach in less than an hour by foot. A deserted old church is all that remains of a village swept away by a hurricane in 1921.

WHERE TO STAY

Crystal Sands Hotel

Canouan, St. Vincent Grenadines

Telephone: (809) 458-8015

Natives of Canouan own and manage this five-duplex cottage resort. The rooms are very basic, each with private bath and paper-thin walls. But if you get one of the three

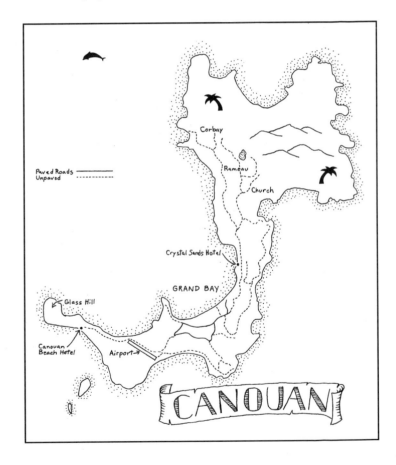

cottages directly on the beach, you will be so entranced with the location, excellent swimming, and friendly fellow guests (usually islanders from St. Vincent), that any inconvenience will quickly be forgotten. Rates start at $110 single and $160 double, including breakfast and dinner.

Canouan Beach Hotel
P.O. Box 530
Canouan, St. Vincent Grenadines
Telephone: (809) 458-8888; fax: (809) 458-8875
Built on the other side of the island from Crystal Sands, the new hotel is so inconspicuous that a visitor could sail into the bay on the interisland boat and miss it entirely. It is French owned, and the international clientele enjoy a wide variety of water sports, snorkeling, and swimming off magnificent, uncrowded beaches. Each of the beachfront bungalows goes for $380, but that includes three meals for two people and most sporting activities.

For visitors on a limited budget, Le Bijou Guest House has six basic rooms on the beach. Breakfast and dinner are included in the $30 single and $60 double rates.

FROM MY JOURNAL

Lots of sun on this dry island. Took an eco-friendly shower and thought that this lack of abundant water is a small price to pay to safeguard Canouan from overdevelopment. We few visitors who do arrive bring contact with the outside world and new jobs for the young, who would otherwise leave the island.

Photo by Burl Willes

Grand Bay, Canouan

HOW TO GET THERE

Boat service from St. Vincent leaves on Monday and Thursday around 9:00 a.m. and arrives on Canouan in the afternoon. The boat returns on Tuesday and Friday. Air Martinique has flights from St. Vincent. If you decide to arrive by sea, reconfirm the boat schedule when making a reservation at your hotel.

PRACTICAL TIPS

Immigration: For Carriacou and Petit Martinique, passports are not required of United States citizens, provided they have two proofs of citizenship (one with photo) and a return air ticket. A driver's license with photo and an original birth certificate will suffice. Be advised that if you visit the St. Vincent Grenadines (Mayreau, Canouan, and Union), you will need a passport. There is an EC$25 (U.S.$9) departure tax when returning to the United States from the Grenada Grenadines and an EC$15 ($6) departure tax from the St. Vincent Grenadines.

Currency: The Eastern Caribbean (EC) dollar is used on all the Grenadine Islands. The exchange rate is approximately EC$2.70 to U.S.$1.

Language: The official language is English.

VENEZUELA

Isla de Coche

Within view of the overdeveloped, heavily touristed Venezuelan resort destination of Isla Margarita lies a remarkable opportunity to get away from it all. Just a 90-minute ferryboat ride or a 20-minute airplane flight from the frantic commercial bustle of Isla Margarita, Isla de Coche offers little more than a supremely tranquil setting for stress-free relaxation at affordable prices. The relatively flat and arid island is home to a thousand or so residents who depend on fishing or intermittent salt manufacturing operations for their living. Tourist development is practically nonexistent—no T-shirts or souvenirs—and it is primarily vacationers from Caracas who cross over from Margarita to check out the absolute peace and quiet of this hidden oasis. But for the adventurous traveler who is looking only for a restful setting to enjoy the sea, the sun, and delicious native cooking, Coche is a rugged chunk of paradise.

Our first sighting of Isla de Coche, from the large passenger ferry that cruises over from Punta de Piedras on Margarita, was ambiguous. From this northerly approach the island appears to be mostly deserted, with a few strange buildings materializing into view. Drawing closer, we saw a string of houses near the long beach to the left of the ferry landing. They are part of a failed housing development near the salt extraction facilities. A huge, concrete, institutional-looking structure on the hill turns out to be the largest of the island's many churches. Initially, the island has a strangely desolate feeling. One or two taxis are waiting at the dock to take passengers on the short trip into San Pedro de Coche, the island's main village. The ride winds through dusty streets, past ramshackle buildings and cinder block housing in various states of construction and disrepair. But once settled into your hotel, with a cool drink and a friendly welcome from the young staff, the foreboding feeling of landing in an alien environment where few tourists tread melts into welcome sighs of relaxation.

Photo by Burl Willes

Vegetation on a Venezuela island

Coche's main appeal is the chance to escape from civilization into a culture that is virtually oblivious to the hyperactivity of mainland life. Add to that the warm and accommodating nature of the other guests (almost all Venezuelan), and what seemed alien becomes comfortable and familiar. The daily life of Coche—the repair of fishing nets and boats, the early morning launches, the preparation of the catch, the late afternoon games in the streets or on the beaches—goes on undisturbed by the trickle of visitors.

Our first walk through the puebla of San Pedro drew silent stares from curious children and bemused adults who rarely see North Americans on their streets. We felt like we had landed from another planet. After exploring the quiet streets of San Pedro, we decided to find a way to investigate the rest of the island. For about $8 an hour, a driver will take you around the entire island—through the smaller villages of Guinima, Guamache, and El Bichar; out past the airport and the salt processing sheds; along the vast white beach at Punta la Playa. If you are lucky, you will hear stories about how the islanders drove a Catholic priest off Coche, because he offended their traditional sensibilities. Taking us back to the 5:00 a.m. ferry on the morning of our departure, our driver, Bertrand, related how he had been visited by spirits in the night, both on the road to Guinima and in his own home. They took the form of nuns and young girls, he said, except for one old woman spirit who is known as "the quiet one."

Our finest hours on Coche were spent swimming in the calm Caribbean waters in the early morning before the considerable heat of noon, or at dusk, when the air is like velvet and large sea birds slant against the crimson and orange, cloud-dappled sky. At night, an unbelievable calm descends with the darkness, even as the evening breezes pick up and rattle the few palms. Sleep comes easily with the gentle rhythms of the waves upon the shore. All the cares you left behind melt away, as Coche reminds you how to lose yourself in the long, peaceful moment.

NOTEWORTHY

Punta la Playa is the location of Coche's finest beach, a long arc of white sand around a cove of warm, shallow water. While you can have immense sections of beach all to yourself, be sure either to bring your own shade (the playa is treeless), or avoid the hot midday hours. Other rockier spots on Coche's shore are excellent for shell collecting.

The Panaderia is a large, relatively modern market pro-

Photo by Burl Willes

Fish explore a reef off Isla de Coche

viding fresh breads, cold drinks, bottled water, and various canned and dry goods. Local fishermen make their boats available for hire. They can take you to the nearby island of Cubagua or to various locations for fishing and snorkeling. Remember, there are no regular tourist services, such as dive shops, on Coche, so it is up to you to find locals who can help you shape your own vacation.

WHERE TO STAY

Hotel Tamarindo Isla de Coche
Isla de Coche via Porlamar, Venezuela
Telephone: (011) 58-95-99-14-15; fax: (011) 58-95-99-11-32
A kind reader alerted us to this new hotel with 23 beachfront cabanas. Daily rates start at $42 per person, including breakfast and dinner, in low season (April 15-December 15), and $52 per person in high season.

There are two budget choices in San Pedro de Coche town, Pension Bija del Rey (on Calle Colon) and Hotel-Restaurante Oea (on Calle San Jose).

RESTAURANTS

Although San Pedro de Coche does have a few tiny bars and markets, the only place to eat is at your hotel or pension, where you are welcome, even if not a guest. The food is excellent. Local women prepare delicious soups with fresh fish, shrimp, and crabs; *arepas* (a fried dough that is sometimes slightly sweet); rice and black beans; fried bananas; and a variety of fish and chicken dishes. The best dinners feature tomato and cheese salads, *tostones* (fried plantain), and *pargo*, a local fish related to grouper and snapper, grilled with garlic. Try the fresh cantalope juice, a delicious and refreshing drink.

If your schedule requires that you spend time on Isla Margarita, take best advantage by enjoying one of the excellent restaurants in Porlamar—such as O Sole Mio Restaurant da Rosetta at Calle Cedeno y Calle Malave, or Restaurant Martin Pescador—that serve enormous portions of delicious lobster in elegant settings at bargain prices.

FROM MY JOURNAL

The door of our small room faces the sea. The palm trees are black silhouettes against an orange sky and the sun lingers above the silver horizon. Children and parents have come to the beach from the village and the nearby fishing huts. Some are swimming, others playing soccer in the sand. A few guests have set up a makeshift volleyball game. A gentle breeze is rustling the palm leaves against the window. The water is like velvet. We look around and see a dozen other bodies half submerged in the warm tide, all motionless, all turned west, away from the beach, staring toward the radiant sunset that is making great pink and purple streaks across the sky.

HOW TO GET THERE

Avensa Air and Linea Aeropostal Venezolana operate scheduled flights from Caracas (Maiquetia Airport) to Isla Margarita. The ferry to Coche departs from Punta de Piedras

Monday through Thursday at 12:30 p.m.; Friday and Saturday at 10:30 a.m.; and Sunday at 8:00 a.m., 1:30 p.m., and 5:30 p.m. But note that schedules can change, and be sure to inquire—preferably in Spanish—about the current times at the terminal. The fare is about $3.

Aero Taxi el Sol de America runs flights from Margarita to Coche twice daily, at 8:00 a.m. and 4:30 p.m., for about $24 per person. But check ahead of time, because the service is not always in operation.

Photo by Derk Richardson

An empty, idyllic beach

Isla de Cubagua

To the east of Isla de Coche lies the smaller island of Isla de Cubagua. The site of the first Spanish city in Venezuela and once the locale of rich pearl fisheries, Cubagua is now a barren and windswept desert island. On Coche you can hear stories about how the Spaniards mercilessly enslaved and murdered the original Indian population and how that original city was swept away centuries ago by a monstrous storm. On Cubagua, you can walk through the rubble of stone that makes up the "ruins" of the early settlement. The only signs of life today are a few shacks used by local fishermen and a small marine laboratory on one of the bays. The island itself is flat and scrubby, its vegetation dominated by several varieties of blooming cactus.

The only way to get to Cubagua is to hire a fishing boat on Coche. Felipe, who lives across the street from the Panaderia, will take you in his partially covered inboard-engine boat for between $35 and $40. You need to leave early in the morning so that you can return before the sea gets rough in the afternoon. The ride takes about an hour and 15 minutes. Two or three hours are enough to explore the ruins, beachcomb, and swim and snorkel around the reefs. The wreck of an old ferry marks the entrance to Ensenada de Charagato. Large gray pelicans roost on the rusted hull. In the quiet bay, sailboats anchor for shelter. It is a fine spot for swimming and shelling, with a smooth sandy beach. On shore, fishermen offered to sell us fresh lobster, but we opted for a shell with a small pearl developing on its inner wall. A truly adventurous soul could probably camp for the night on Cubagua, but a day trip is enough for a glimpse of a place where the distant past and the present are not very far apart.

Los Roques

The archipelago of Los Roques has a rather dramatic way of introducing itself. Flying from Maiquetia airport on the Venezuelan coast in a little 20-seater plane, the first thing most visitors see is a pencil-thin line in the distance, a slight break in the monotony of the Caribbean's slate blue surface. A few minutes later you can see that the line is a boundary between the slate blue and a startlingly brilliant expanse of aqua water beyond—water dotted with flat atolls that are ringed by the whitest beaches you've ever seen. Welcome to Los Roques.

A trip to these islands is anything but a typical tourist experience. Development is forbidden here, because the archipelago was designated a national park in 1972, so there are no high-rise hotels lined up along the beach. In fact, there are no hotels at all, only rooms for rent and a fishing lodge. Because of its status as a park, it is also against the law to tamper with Los Roques' marine life or take souvenirs, so the beaches and reefs remain pristine.

The number of visitors is limited by the islands' remoteness (about 70 miles off the mainland) and lack of

Photo by Eileen Ecklund

Fishing boats, El Gran Roque

facilities, and by the fact that there isn't much information about them available outside of Venezuela. (The government's famed inefficiency extends to its promotion of tourism; their loss is our gain.) Most tourists come over on day trips from Caracas or Margarita Island; few stay overnight. It's quite possible to stay overnight, though; and once you're there, you'll probably want to spend a week exploring the 360-odd islands and cays that make up the park (only about 50 islands are large enough to have names). The archipelago comprises 556,345 acres, with coral reefs, cays, and shallow lagoons formed by the 15-mile-long, arc-shaped barrier reef that you see from the plane. Some of the "islands" peek up out of the water only at low tide.

The islands are flat and quite arid, with the exception of the largest (it's still less than a mile long), El Gran Roque, which has a spine of steep, rocky ridges. There isn't much vegetation other than the mangrove trees that stud many of the inlets, although desertlike plants grow along the ridges of El Gran Roque, and palms have been planted around its town. This tiny town is the only one in Los Roques; its residents depend on fishing and tourists for their living. There are a few fishermen's huts on some of the other cays. While there may not be many human inhabitants in Los Roques, there's no lack of marine life—the red coral reefs are famed for their abundance of colorful fish and plants. Bonefish are popular with the sport fishermen, while the locals fish for red snapper, grouper, mackerel, and, in season, lobster. In addition, bird-watchers come from all over to spot the more than 45 species of birds. Iguanas, black salamanders, and turtles are also common sights. A Venezuelan scientific foundation has a research site at Dos Mosquises, which you can visit.

Because there are no commercial airline flights to Los Roques, and no hotels once you arrive, most visitors make arrangements beforehand with one of the private tour companies operating on the islands. Although this is by far the easiest way to go, there's no guarantee it will be trouble-free. The first time we tried to schedule a visit, the islanders went on strike to demand that the Venezuelan government make good on its promises of a dependable water supply, and all the tourists had to be hauled back to the mainland.

Once we made it to Los Roques, though, we were pampered from start to finish. The minute we stepped off the plane at the tiny landing strip, we were greeted by our host, walked to our lodging, and brought a cooler full of drinks. In the evening we were taken to dinner, and in the morning, shooed off to breakfast before our scheduled boat tour. All of this could be oppressive, but it's not. You're pretty much left alone when you want to be; the hosts are friendly, helpful, and full of information; and you can tailor your visit any way you'd like with the company's help.

The day after we arrived, we found ourselves scheduled for a tour by catamaran, provided by the company as part of the room package. Fortified by tiny cups of the excellent, strong Venezuelan coffee, we set off in the morning, to explore some cays. Stopping at Cayo Francés after about an hour on the water, we spent several hours

Photo by Eileen Ecklund

Relaxing at Cayo Francés

swimming, strolling, and lounging in the shade of the temporary shelters. Poking around at the shells and coral that litter the beach, we found that the dazzling white sand, which is actually pulverized coral and has the consistency of powdered sugar, sticks to you like a second layer of skin. In the afternoon we took off in the small launch with a few others to snorkel at a nearby red coral reef, which also sported a tiny pink sand beach. The views both below and above the water were fantastic here. Below, enormous tropically hued fish swam lazily around huge outcrops of red coral and banks of flowery anemones; while on the surface, the expanse of water shaded from deep blue to bright green in bands, as the depth of the water changed.

If you want an afternoon off from exploring by boat, you can walk around town on El Gran Roque. It's a rare chance to see traditional, brightly painted Venezuelan houses that are in good repair. The pretty little houses are shaded by some of the islands' few (imported) trees. You can also take a longer hike up to the remains of an old lighthouse on a nearby ridge. There is no dive shop on Los Roques, so if you plan to dive, you have to make arrangements for equipment on the mainland. If you go with one of the tour companies, they can handle all the details for you and will even provide a guide. The companies also provide snorkeling equipment.

There's also no nightlife or culture to speak of here; dinner with several other guests in the communal dining area is the main socializing event. After long days in the hot sun, though, relaxation is what you'll most likely have in mind. We spent evenings chatting with the other people in our house (a scuba diving couple from New York and an

Italian family currently living in Brazil), reading a book, or just sitting on the porch, drink in hand, listening to the surf.

NOTEWORTHY

Cayo Francés, Blackman's Cay, and Cayo Sal are all recommended for snorkeling and scuba diving, as is the islands' central lagoon, Ensenada de los Corales. Near Cayo Francés, a barely submerged shoal extends far out into the water; you can wade out knee-deep for what seems like miles. Cayo Francés is also a hot spot for bird-watching, as is Cayo Bobo Negro.

WHERE TO STAY

Your choices are limited when it comes to accommodations in Los Roques. The tour groups that operate on the islands own a few guesthouses in which you can book a room, and some of the residents rent rooms in their own houses. There are also rooms at the Los Roques Light Tackle Club, a privately owned fisherman's club, or you can camp or stay on a boat. It's sometimes possible to find a less expensive room by asking around once you get to El Gran Roque, but the total number of rooms on the island is small. Your best bet is to make reservations ahead of time, or you may find yourself stuck there with no place to stay and no available seats for the return flight to Caracas.

You can make arrangements on the mainland through any Venezuelan tour agency, or you can talk directly to the tour groups that operate on Los Roques. The main ones are Aereotuy (02-716-231) and Cave (02-952-1806), and their prices for rooms range from $60 to $150. These prices typically include food, drinks, and one boat excursion.

The guesthouse we stayed in on Los Roques, owned by the Aereotuy company, was typical of the lodging you'll find there—very nice, though more like a rustic beach house than standard hotel fare. It was spacious and cool, with cement floors and an open air porch just a few feet from the sea, ceiling fans, a large living room and kitchen area (including refrigerator), and a shower with cold water only, which is all you're likely to need in this balmy climate. It had three sizable rooms, the largest of which had its own bath.

There's no real restaurant and no market on the islands (provisions, including water, must be brought in from

Photo by Eileen Ecklund

A typical wood-barred house, El Gran Roque

the mainland), but food and drinks are generally included in the price of a room. It's always a good idea to bring extra drinking water, however. Aereotuy, the group we went with, maintains its own kitchen and dining facilities, and hires residents to cook for its guests. The food we had was excellent and plentiful, consisting primarily of fresh fish prepared in a variety of ways.

Several tour groups offer overnight stays on boats. The Caracas tour agency that booked our trip, Alpi Tours (02-283-1433), has a number of yachts for both day trips and overnight stays.

FROM MY JOURNAL

With the sun just beginning to sink into the Caribbean, we sit on the porch of our house, a few feet from the water, and watch the pelicans fish. One big fellow perches on the prow of a nearby boat to gulp down his catch. Fishing boats are coming in for the night, their bright paint made even gaudier by the colors of the setting sun.

As I wade out into the warm water to catch the evening's cooling breeze, a young boy comes walking down the beach carrying four fish that are almost as big as he is. Jumping at his heels, a couple of puppies tumble each other into the waves and coat themselves with sand. Everything is utterly peaceful; it feels as if life hasn't changed much here for the past 100 years, and it probably hasn't. I turn to go back into the house and stumble over a huge, perfect pink-and-white conch shell left to lie on the beach. As my eyes grow accustomed to the fading light, I spot another, and another, and another.

HOW TO GET THERE

The charter tour companies of Aereotuy and Cave (see "Where to Stay," above) are the primary flight operators to Los Roques; round-trip tickets on either cost $100. Both have flights leaving for the islands from the domestic terminal in Maiquetia several times daily, weekends included. The small planes used for the 35-minute flight can't carry much weight, so pack lightly.

The other option is to charter a boat or book passage on one of the yachts or sailboats operated by tour groups. It takes eight to ten hours to reach Los Roques by boat.

Isla de Plata, Mono, and Chimana Grande

One of Venezuela's most beautiful coastal areas is Mochima National Park, between the cities of Puerto La Cruz and Cumana, about 200 miles east of Caracas. In Mochima, steep mountains covered with lush tropical vegetation sweep down to the palm tree-shaded beaches rimming the Caribbean, while just offshore, craggy islands poke their heads out of the sea.

These islands, uninhabited except for a few fishermen who were allowed to stay on when the park was created, are largely rocky and arid, with deep coves, coral reefs, lagoons surrounded by mangroves, and a few tiny beaches. While it can be fun to spend a day exploring the dozen or so islands within the park's boundaries, there are three that really stand out as worth a return visit: Isla de Plata, Mono, and Chimana Grande.

A ten-minute boat ride from Puerto Guanta (near Puerto La Cruz) on the mainland, tiny Isla de Plata has one large beach shaded by palms. Our first sight of the island was a contrast in colors: the brilliant blue of the water; the cheery red, orange, and blue of the covered beach chairs

Chimana Grande's palapa-studded beach

sprouting from the white sand; the deep green of the palms hovering above. Once ashore, the view back toward the mainland was equally eye-catching, with the mountains looming out of the sea, lost in fog and clouds at their peaks. Unfortunately, the view in one direction is marred by a huge concrete plant hunkered down on the mainland waterfront.

A popular spot with local residents as well as tourists, Plata is often crowded and boisterous, with children splashing in the surf, teenagers playing paddleball on the beach, and adults drowsing in the sun. The island's one restaurant hosts whole families who crowd around tables eating filled *arepas* and other Venezuelan specialties, while young men in bathing trunks belly up to the bar for a Polar, the country's most popular beer. After a few hours of soaking up sun and swimming in the shallow, warm water, we took off for

Photo by Eileen Ecklund

nearby Mono. Although it is larger than Plata, Mono's rocky cliffs and dense, scrubby vegetation make inland exploration next to impossible. Skirting its edges, we first came on a large, very deep protected bay, which, according to our guide, is a popular spot with local fishermen.

Pointing to several makeshift shelters perched on the surrounding cliffs, the guide explained that they shade the lookouts, who are stationed there to spot schools of fish through the crystal clear waters. When the fishermen aren't in residence, this spot is also excellent for snorkeling and scuba diving; you have to dive from the boat, though, as there is no landing.

Our next stop was Mono's tiny, pristine beach. As we came in to dock at the one little pier, the view was dominated by a large, ramshackle wood house clinging dramatically, if somewhat precariously, to a cliff at the opposite side of the beach. A little open air restaurant was sheltered beneath the cliff on which the house was perched. Clambering ashore, we found only one other sunbather enjoying the beauties of this secluded spot, even though it was a Saturday afternoon.

The beach's "host," relaxing in a chair outside the restaurant, hauled out his own photo album as soon as he saw us snapping pictures, and we spent an hour or so admiring his photography and attempting to chat in our very limited Spanish. Because Mono is farther from the mainland and its beach is so small, it has fewer visitors than Isla de Plata, although it, too, fills up during Venezuelan holidays. Just off the beach is an expanse of coral reefs that make for good snorkeling, particularly along the cliffs. There is no shade on the beach itself, though you can get some relief from the sun inside the restaurant or under a few trees set back against the cliffs. All in all, it's a peaceful, pleasant place in which to laze away an afternoon.

Caught up in exploring these islands, we postponed our trip to the Chimana group for another day. Farther off the coast, these islands are best reached by boat from Puerto La Cruz itself or from the resort marina to the west of the city.

While there are a number of islands in this group, the largest, Chimana Grande, is the main destination. On one side of the island is a large cove ringed by rocky cliffs, with a small mangrove lagoon at one end. Joining several other boats that were already anchored in the cove, we took turns piloting the dinghy around the shore and through the mangroves, where there is a spectacular array of marine life. Making our way around the other side of Chimana Grande, we found a large beach, Playa El Saco, with palm-thatched sun shelters and a large open air restaurant for visitors. Trails run up to a ridge behind the beach, where there's a lookout point with a fabulous view of the mainland beyond and along the cliffs to one side of it.

At El Saco's dock, we were greeted by the imposing figure of Luis Leatán, one of the beach's hosts. Standing with feet planted wide on the pier and arms akimbo, necklaces of shell and coral strung across his bare chest, with a red bandana on top of his head and a huge, fierce mustache drooping down his chin, Luis looked like nothing so much as a Caribbean pirate. First impressions aside, he turned out to be one of the friendliest souls we met.

Under Luis's guidance, we discovered what El Saco has to offer. In addition to its obvious attractions (the beach, the water sports, the view from the lookout), this corner of Chimana Grande is also a great place for spotting iguanas, which hide among its rocky, cactus-strewn slopes. Skirting the tops of the cliffs, you can look straight down through the brilliant blue water to the coral reefs below, with their array of fish, eels, and other marine life. After hiking around for a while in the hot sun, it's a relief to relax on the restaurant's shaded patio, sip drinks, and swap stories with Luis and other visitors.

The restaurant and cabanas at El Saco were built by the Doral Beach Resort, which offers excursions to the Chimanas; the beach is often referred to now as Doral Beach. In addition to day trips from Puerto La Cruz, you can arrange special package trips to El Saco, like overnight camping excursions (food and drinking water included) or a "tropical fiesta" evening, which includes a buffet meal and dancing to a steel band.

Although it's hardly an isolated spot, Chimana Grande is far enough from the mainland to avoid overcrowding. Because they are part of a national park, none of the islands we visited in Mochima have any of the typical tourist trappings, like T-shirt or souvenir stands; development is limited to beach shelters and small restaurants. The atmosphere is, as Luis Leatán would say, "muy simpatico."

WHERE TO STAY

There are no accommodations on any of the islands in Mochima National Park, although you can make arrangements to camp. Nearby Puerto La Cruz is the place to stay if you want a hotel or a room in a guesthouse. One of

Luis Leatán on Chimana Grande

Venezuela's premier tourist cities, as well as a shipping and commercial center, Puerto La Cruz is crowded with visitors, mostly from Europe, Canada, and Venezuela itself. The boulevard that runs along the harbor, the Paseo Colón, is jammed with traffic during the day and on weekend evenings. Still, Puerto La Cruz is a pleasant city and moderately priced for its location. Most visitors choose to stay along the waterfront, and for good reason. A wide, shaded pedestrian walkway runs parallel to Paseo Colón along the beach, affording views of palm trees, white sand, and deep blue Caribbean waters. In the evening, a mild breeze comes up as vacationers stroll among the artisans' stalls, wander down to the water's edge, or watch the sun set and boat lights wink on, while sipping cocktails on the patio of one of several restaurant/cafés.

Accommodations in Puerto La Cruz range from budget to five-star. Hotel prices are cheaper in the city proper than in the tourist district, but it's still possible to find a nice room for a reasonable rate on the waterfront.

Hotel Riviera
Paseo Colón No. 33
Puerto La Cruz, Venezuela
Telephone: (58) 081-22268; fax: (58) 081-691337
Despite its name, the Riviera isn't fancy, but it does have comfortable, air-conditioned rooms, a staff that's friendly and helpful, and a location that can't be beat. It's right across the street from the beach. Rooms start at $28.

RESTAURANTS

Puerto La Cruz, vacation spot that it is, has no lack of excellent restaurants. There are several waterfront restaurants on the Paseo Colón that, even though somewhat overpriced, offer good fresh seafood, open air dining, and a magnificent view. Tascas sprinkled throughout the tourist district serve Spanish-style food, including marvelous seafood paellas. One of the best is El Parador, on Paseo Colón.

We highly recommend the Casa Pueblo (Calle Carabobo just off Paseo Colón), which serves traditional Venezuelan food, like grilled seafood and steaks, roast chicken with a caper and raisin gravy, fried plantains, and *pabellon*, a dish of minced beef and beans. Prices are a middle-range $5 to $8 a person for a huge plate of food, and you can listen to the band playing Latin music as you dine.

FROM MY JOURNAL

As we set out for the islands in the early morning light, sipping coffee and trying to shake off our lethargy, a school of flying fish suddenly skims past the bow, sending drops of water skittering in its path. That does the trick: we're all awake now, pointing, laughing, and hoping to see more. Soon someone spots a rainbow-colored lump in the clear water just off the side of the boat. It's a big jellyfish, tentacles dangling behind, and it's not long before we're accustomed to the sight—they're everywhere. Later, in the heat of the afternoon, we return to the boat from snorkeling among the mangroves to find cool drinks awaiting us. Soon, most of us are dozing, using hats, towels, and whatever else we can find to ward off the sun. Toward evening, it clouds over and spatters us with a light rain, but as we return at dusk, the sky clears for one of those marvelous sunsets, and we return to the harbor as the lights are beginning to twinkle on in the deep purple glow.

HOW TO GET THERE

Linea Aeropostal Venezolana operates ten daily flights from Caracas (Maiquetia Airport) to the city of Barcelona, next to Puerto La Cruz; the price is $50 round trip.

From Puerto La Cruz, you have numerous options for renting boats to the islands, which are just offshore. On Paseo Colón, the beachfront strip in downtown Puerto La Cruz, you can ask any of the boat operators to take you out. A trip to Chimana Grande costs about $5. You can also make arrangements with a company called Transtupaco, which was recommended as "reliable," for about the same price. Some of the nearby resort hotels also offer day tours by yacht, with prices ranging from $30 to $60.

To get to Isla de Plata and Mono, your best bet is to take a bus or taxi to the harbor of nearby Puerto Guanta, where you can catch a taxi boat to Plata for a few dollars. Or hire your own guide to take you to Mono and some of the other outlying islands for a few dollars more.

PRACTICAL TIPS

Immigration: A passport is required for entrance into Venezuela; a visa is not necessary, but a tourist card is. Tourist cards are free and can be obtained from the airline or from immigration on landing in Caracas. You should keep your passport and tourist card with you at all times.

Currency: The Venezuelan currency is based on the bolivar (B). At the time of publication, the standard exchange rate was 170 B to the dollar. Prices in Venezuela are on the rise, particularly for food, transportation, and lodging, but are still quite reasonable. You can get an excellent meal for less than U.S.$10, and good accommodations for about U.S.$20. The best places to change money are at the international airport terminal near Caracas or at the Italcambios in Caracas. Both of these also cash traveler's checks, which otherwise can be difficult to exchange.

Traveling: In-country flights in Venezuela are often reasonably priced, but fares to popular or remote destinations run higher. Buses, boats, and the Caracas Metro are still very cheap, while taxis tend to be overpriced but still affordable.

If you fly, be aware that you will have to pay an airport tax of $4 to $5 before boarding; you must also pay an exit tax when you leave Venezuela. Ask where the tax booth is located when you check in at the airline counter. You must also confirm all airline reservations in advance, either by fax or in writing. Confirm return reservations as soon as you arrive at your destination. You don't always need advance reservations to fly, but if you're headed for a popular destination, you may spend a long time at the airport waiting for a seat. Flights rarely leave on time.

Accommodations: Avoid so-called luxury accommodations in Venezuela; they're seldom worth the price. In many parts of the country there are government-subsidized Corporturismo hotels that cost about $20 per person, are pleasant and clean, and have hot running water. Some charge slightly higher prices for foreigners.

Health: Especially when visiting islands and beaches, always take a hat, sunscreen, and plenty of bottled water. The sun is intense, and there is often no shade. Bottled water isn't available everywhere, and tap water should be avoided.

BELIZE

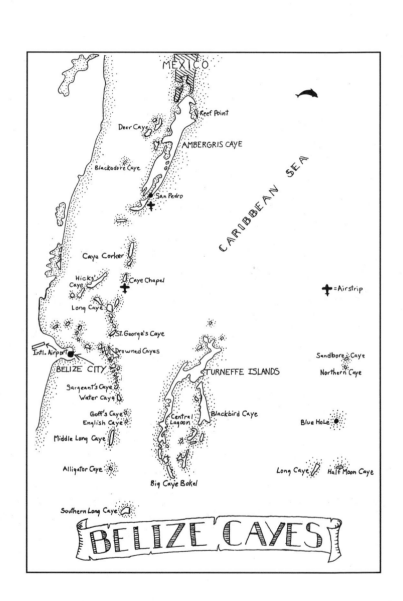

MEXICO

Reef Point

Deer Caye

AMBERGRIS CAYE

Blackadore Caye

San Pedro

Caye Corker

Hicks' Caye

Caye Chapel

✝ =Airstrip

Long Caye

St. George's Caye

Intl. Airport

Drowned Cayes

BELIZE CITY

Sargeant's Caye
Water Caye

Goff's Caye
English Caye

Middle Long Caye

Alligator Caye

Southern Long Caye

CARIBBEAN SEA

TURNEFFE ISLANDS

Central Lagoon

Blackbird Caye

Big Caye Bokel

Sandbore Caye
Northern Caye

Blue Hole

Long Caye   Half Moon Caye

BELIZE CAYES

Formerly British Honduras and now a member of the British Commonwealth as an independent democratic nation, Belize is unique among Central American countries. It is an uncrowded country of only 15 inhabitants per square mile. When the nonprofit Freedom House Foundation ranked countries according to their respect for human rights and civil liberties, it grouped Belize with Britain, Canada, and the United States. It is a safe and stable country with a literacy rate of more than 90 percent. The friendly and hospitable English-speaking inhabitants welcome visitors warmly and are striving to develop a tourist industry to boost their declining sugar-based economy.

Although primitive in some ways, Belize is both healthy and safe. Water is drinkable almost everywhere, and inoculations are unnecessary. For a poor country, there is a remarkable lack of theft and panhandling. The people are friendly, helpful, and proud. There are 175 islands off the coast of Belize! These beautiful cayes (pronounced "keys") are flat, narrow, beach-lined islands that are mostly populated by an incredible variety of birds. Less than a dozen cayes have any human inhabitants, and aside from several privately owned resort islands and various research stations, only four cayes offer overnight accommodations. No other island group in the Caribbean has a larger or more spectacular barrier reef than Belize's, which is second in size only to the Great Barrier Reef of Australia.

Ambergris Caye, sharing a border with Mexico's Yucatán, is the most developed. Just south is Caye Caulker (pronounced and sometimes spelled "Caye Corker"). Here one can stay for as little as $15 a night or "splurge" on a hearty lobster dinner for $8! St. George's Caye is home to a few residents, and two small cottage "resorts." There are several lodges on private cayes: Turneffe Island Lodge on Caye Bokel; Manta Resort on Glover's Reef; Pyramid Island Resort on Caye Chapel; the Wave Hotel on Gallows Point Caye; and Blue Marlin Lodge and Leslie Cottager on South Water Caye. These isolated lodges are known only to the most avid scuba divers and fishermen, who have found these waters to be among the world's finest diving and fishing destinations. Those who bemoan the increasing popularity of Caye Caulker, with its new Band-aid-sized airstrip, will want to turn back the clock and head directly to Tobacco Caye.

If time allows, visits to the Mayan sites of Xunantunich and Altun Ha on the mainland (and especially Tikal in Guatemala) are richly rewarding. Belize is a natural wonder, supporting more than 500 species of exotic birds and 250 varieties of orchids. It is one of the last stands of the elusive jaguar.

Ambergris Caye

Many new, small guesthouses and hotels have opened on Ambergris in the last few years. Some would say too many have opened, but buildings are still restricted to no more than three stories in height, and they have not spoiled the sleepy atmosphere of this 35-mile-long island. There may now be an air-conditioned luxury hotel or two, but the streets—Front, Middle, and Back—remain nothing more than hard-packed white sand. Automobiles are still rare.

San Pedro, the island's only town, has a white, dusty frontier look about it. The wooden buildings are parched and weathered by the salt and searing sun. Fishing still remains the island's chief concern, but tourism has brought employment and income to many who would otherwise have left the island. After a bountiful catch, picturesque fishing boats line the waterfront of San Pedro town. Fresh fish grilled to perfection is one of the joys of an Ambergris stay.

Here on Ambergris the reef is less than a mile offshore, and the waves can be seen breaking easily along it. The pristine and virgin quality of the reef make it one of the world's best diving locations. Massive coral canyons at

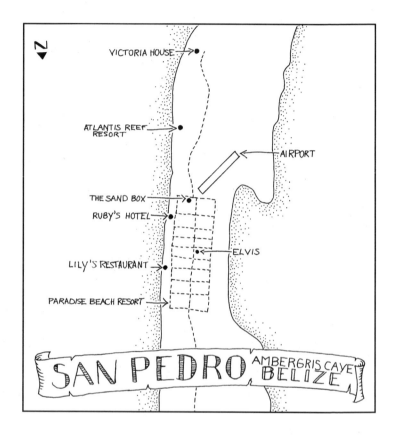

N

VICTORIA HOUSE

ATLANTIS REEF RESORT

AIRPORT

THE SAND BOX

RUBY'S HOTEL

ELVIS

LILY'S RESTAURANT

PARADISE BEACH RESORT

SAN PEDRO, AMBERGRIS CAYE, BELIZE

depths of 50 to 100 feet can be explored along the main barrier reef. Each canyon is full of caves and tunnels teeming with life, and it is not unusual to see a school of porpoises or huge turtles swimming along beside you.

Time moves slowly on Ambergris. Dogs sleep at high noon on the sandy main street. Toward evening they amble aside for the San Pedro youngsters playing softball. Fishing, swimming, snorkeling, scuba diving, sailing, eating, reading, sleeping; there is much to be said for this island's lazy and rejuvenating way of life.

NOTEWORTHY

Marine life is decreasing on Ambergris, except at the Hol Chan Marine Reserve, a four-square-mile area at the south end of the caye which opened as a national park in May 1987. This spectacular area has been set aside for the protection and observation of marine life and will become a major spawning area for hundreds of fish species. Calm and protected, the water is a wonderland of brilliantly colored fish of fluorescent orange and purple, dazzling red and green, and electric blue.

WHERE TO STAY

Paradise Resort Hotel
San Pedro, Ambergris Caye, Belize
Telephone: (011) 501-26-2083; fax: (011) 501-26-2232
The Paradise is the nicest hotel right in town. Thatch-roofed cottages are arranged around a beachfront garden with bar and lounge areas. Rates start at $40 single, $65 double; air-conditioned suites are $100. Excellent food.

Rubie's Hotel
San Pedro, Ambergris Caye, Belize
Telephone: (011) 501-26-2063
This budget hotel has no air conditioning and no frills, but it is right on the beach, with good ventilation and superb views in two directions. Rates range from $12.50 to $35 per night.

San Pedro's serene waterfront

Photo by Vincent Costa

Royal Palm

P.O. Box 18
San Pedro, Ambergris Caye, Belize
Telephone: (011) 501-26-2148; fax: (011) 501-26-2329
These 12 new villas with pool have opened since our last
visit. They are in a good beachfront location near the Victoria
House.

Victoria House

P.O. Box 22
San Pedro, Ambergris Caye, Belize
Telephone: (011) 501-26-2067; fax: (011) 501-26-2429;
U.S. telephone: (800) 247-5159
About a mile south of San Pedro, there are ten very com-

fortable, small, thatch-roofed casitas and 11 deluxe air-conditioned rooms in the main lodge. A lovely old plantation house faces the nicest beach on the island. Rates range from $120 to $170. Two- and three-bedroom houses are also available. Add $35 per person for three meals a day.

HOUSEKEEPING APARTMENTS

Mata Rocks Resort
P.O. Box 47
San Pedro, Ambergris Caye, Belize
Telephone: (011) 501-26-2336; fax: (011) 501-26-2349
U.S. reservations: (800) 288-8646; fax: (503) 690-9308
There are nine deluxe suites, all with kitchens and a choice of air conditioning or ceiling fans, at this pleasant small resort 1.2 miles south of San Pedro. The Squirrel's Nest Bar serves lunch and tropical drinks in a beachfront setting. Rates range from $85 to $125, plus service charge and tax.

RESTAURANTS

Elvi's, a sand-floored hut on the center street of town, features inexpensive local seafood with conch and lobster specialties. Sand Box is a good Mexican restaurant across the road from the airport in San Pedro town.

The Hut, a moderately priced popular restaurant, is noted for its turtle curry. Owner Shelley Prevett provides hard-to-get information (about babysitters, air charters, local black coral jewelry makers, etc.). Shelly's brother, Penny Arceo, is a knowledgeable instructor of bonefishing, snorkeling, diving, and bird-watching.

Lily's in San Pedro still serves the best breakfast and best seafood in town.

HOW TO GET THERE

American Airlines and TACA International operate nonstop service from Miami (two hours). TACA also serves Houston and New Orleans. Maya and Tropic Air fly to San Pedro from Belize City. Now that Belize and Guatemala are on friendly terms, one can fly from Belize City to Flores (45 minutes) and drive from there to the spectacular Mayan site of Tikal (45 minutes by bus or jeep rented from Flores Airport). One-day packages are available in Belize City. It is quite feasible to drive to Belize City from any point in the United States, then leave the car behind for the ferry trip to Ambergris, Caye Caulker, or St. George Caye.

Boats leave from Shell Station in Belize City, $15 nonstop. From Southern Foreshore Jetty, boats leave for San Pedro Monday-Friday at 4 p.m. and return at 7 a.m. The Saturday departure is 1 p.m., return 8 a.m.

Caye Caulker

A few miles south of Ambergris is less visited and less expensive Caye Caulker. The island is so narrow that you can see the water on the other side as you approach one of the little docks that the locals call "bridges." The caye is virtually all beach, and the inhabited portion is so small that one can easily walk its length and breadth within an hour. It is a barefoot island; all the roads and paths are sand, free of rocks and broken glass. After a day or two, one gets to know many of the 450 friendly islanders and the visitors who come from all parts of the world. Local artist Phillip Lewis, whose work decorates the face of Belizean currency, still manages to update his indispensable map, even though he has moved to Switzerland (we hope temporarily!). The hand-drawn, user-friendly map includes everything from where to get a massage, to the entrance of the world's largest underwater cave system. Also included are the many new, small restaurants that have opened since our last visit. The friendliness and low prices of Caye Caulker tempt the visitor into long stays.

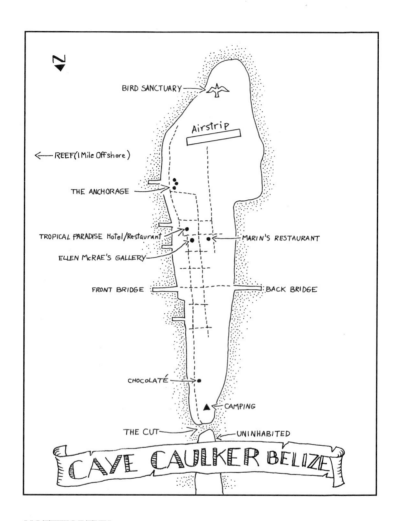

NOTEWORTHY

Ellen MacRae's Art Gallery: Ellen MacRae is not only a fine graphic artist, but also a marine biologist who lectures on reef ecology and bird-watching. If the conditions are right, she will follow her lecture with a guided trip to the reef.

The Cut: This deep channel slices through the island and is an ideal place for swimming, especially since much of the water around the island is so shallow. It is a local favorite for children, who enjoy the high diving from the branch of an overhanging tree.

Lobster traps near Marin's

WHERE TO STAY

Marin's Hotel
Caye Caulker, Belize
Telephone: (011) 501-224-4307
You are greeted with a very warm welcome at this clean and comfortable courtyard inn. Rooms with private bath start at $30 per couple.

Tropical Paradise Hotel and Beach Cottages
Ramon Reyes Street
Caye Caulker, Belize
Telephone: (011) 501-22-2124
Toward the south end of the village on the reef (east) side, the Tropical Paradise now has three new luxury cabanas with air conditioning, refrigerator, and television: $60 for two, and $70 for four. Other cabanas with fan and private bath start at $45 for two.

RESTAURANTS

Marin's: The delicious lobster, served indoors or out in the garden, is as good as any outside of Maine. Two large tails with hot butter cost only $5. They were so tasty that, even though I went back three times, I could never get myself to try anything else!

Tropical Paradise Hotel Restaurant: This is the place to go for breakfast or lunch. You eat in the sunny courtyard or inside, where ceiling fans keep it pleasantly cool. My favorites are their conch fritters, which cost only $1 for a plate of two—they're the size of hamburgers but are much more satisfying.

HOW TO GET THERE

Morning boats from Belize City make the journey in about an 1½ hours. At Mom's Triangle Inn (a famous rendezvous spot), tour and boat information is posted on a bulletin board. Chocolat, who runs a boat to and from Caye Caulker every day except Sunday, can be found eating breakfast there every morning. He charges about $6 for one-way passage on the Soledad, his open boat that bounces like a roller coaster as it speeds over the waves. Mangrove islets appear through the salty spray as the mainland vanishes from view. Coming from nearby Ambergris, you can charter a boat for the short trip.

Tropic Air, Island Air and Maya Air fly from Belize City municipal airport. Cost is $36 round trip, and $50 from the international airport.

PRACTICAL TIPS

Travelers of all nationalities need passports, as well as sufficient funds and an onward ticket.

There is a $12 international departure tax.

The monetary unit is the Belizean dollar, stabilized at BZ $2 to U.S.$1.

Mosquito repellant is important, especially December-February.

St. George's Caye

Less than nine miles from Belize City Harbor, St. George's Caye was the first capital of British Honduras from 1650 to 1784. It is reputed to be the scene of a great sea battle against the Spaniards in 1798, which ended in British possession of the country. With only a small resident population, the island is much quieter today, and only a few reminders of its past endure. A sandy footpath parallels the coastline from the public pier. The swimming and snorkeling are excellent from any of the seven piers, or "bridges." Most of the spectacular dive sites are only ten to 15 minutes from the dock of the island's only lodge.

WHERE TO STAY

St. George's Lodge
P.O. Box 625
Belize City, Belize
Telephone: (011) 501-244-190;
U.S. telephone: (800) 678-6871
The oldest accommodation on the island, St. George's Lodge is a secluded retreat handcrafted of local hard-

woods. The beamed cathedral ceiling and handmade furniture in the public area are unique. The lodge has ten rooms in the main building and six thatch-roofed cottages built over the ocean.

St. George's specializes in scuba diving certification and is the only official Nitrox center in Belize. The two-dive-a-day package, which includes transfers, meals, gratuities, and taxes, is $249 a day per person. The non-dive daily rate is $189. Both require a three-night minimum stay.

Cottage Colony
P.O. Box 428
Belize City, Belize
Telephone: (011) 501-27-7051; fax: (011) 501-27-3253
These pleasant, colonial-style cabanas opened in 1993 and offer travelers a less expensive alternative on St. George's Caye.

HOW TO GET THERE

Occasional boats from Belize City make the 20-minute crossing to the public pier, but most visitors are guests at the island's accommodations and are met by private boat.

Tobacco Caye

W hen life gets too frantic for artist Phillip Lewis, he dreams of Tobacco Caye. We never promised to keep Tobacco Caye a secret, but we probably would have if the island had been easier to reach, or if it had been any larger than a few acres of sand and coconut palms. This dream escape from civilization, with its reef just wading distance offshore, is worth the extra effort to get there. The friendly local families who have started two guesthouses and a tent camp are anxious for a few more visitors—added income that would mean success for their hard work.

WHERE TO STAY

Reef's End Lodge
P.O. Box 10
Dangriga, Belize
Telephone: (011) 501-52-2142
Nolan and Winnie Jackson welcome guests to their small, solar-powered inn located at the far south end of the island. Each of the four rooms has a double bed and its own private bath. The daily rate of $65 per person includes

Life in the Tobacco Caye fast lane

three Belizean-style meals, which are served in their kitchen built over the sea, on the edge of the reef. There is excellent snorkeling right off the sand.

Fairweather & Friends

P.O. Box 240

Belize City, Belize

Mr. Elwood Fairweather, who also owns one of the boats that provide transportation to the island, runs this six-room beachfront inn. He can arrange an economical three-day package to include transportation, room, and meals.

Island Camps

P.O. Box 174, 51 Regent Street

Belize City, Belize

Telephone: (011) 501-27-2109

Owner Mark Bradley will pick up guests in Dangriga. His campground is neat and spacious. Meals and reef excursions can be arranged.

HOW TO GET THERE

Dangriga, 105 miles from Belize City, is the departure port for Tobacco Caye. There is no regular boat service to the island, but your guesthouse or campground can make boat reservations for you. The cost is approximately $88 each way. If you prefer to make your own reservations or wait to share a boat, call 5-22142 or 5-22419.

Gallows Point Caye

Only seven miles by boat from Belize City, Gallows Point Caye is one of the most beautiful and unspoiled cayes in the western Caribbean. For those lucky enough to stay here or just visit for the day, it is never crowded. There is only one small hotel on the four-mile-long, 300-acre, privately owned island, just one-half mile from the Barrier Reef.

WHERE TO STAY

The Wave Hotel
9 Regent Street West
Belize City, Belize
Telephone: (011) 501-27-3054
All six rooms with private baths (cold-water showers) are on the second floor off a sea view veranda. A single is $87, a double, $120, which includes three meals and transport from Belize City. Rustic, shared-bath accommodations and breakfast in the Weir House is $35 per night. Day trips are available for about $35, diving trips for $60.

WEST CARIBBEAN

Isla Mujeres

Change comes slowly to Isla Mujeres. Although the "Island of Women" is just a short boat ride away from the plastic glamour and programmed vacationland of Cancún, it resists the invasion of high-rise hotels and shopping malls. Isla Mujeres may be one of the least hidden of the Caribbean's hidden islands, as more and more North Americans and Europeans discover its charms, but it still exists as a world apart from the luxury hotels and designer luggage across the water.

The narrow, five-mile-long island sustains an extraordinary balance of tourism and the authentic indigenous life of a Mexican fishing village. Although large parties of Cancúnites cruise over on tour boats for day trips of snorkeling and buffets, they usually stay away from the town in their preplanned outings. And while certain omens of modernization have crept in—satellite television dishes at a few bars, air conditioning in several hotels—there are some signs of deferred progress. Small plane service from the Cancún airport to the Isla Mujeres army base airstrip has been discontinued, and the boldest attempt at a high-rise luxury hotel is already looking a bit weather-beaten in its isolated location at the northern tip of the island (it was closed in January 1995 with no immediate plans to reopen as a hotel). New construction proceeds very slowly, and it is visually offset by the older, timeworn architecture and tempered by the leisurely pace of life determined by geography and climate. So Isla Mujeres is not overwhelmed by rampant growth, and its attractions of gorgeous beaches, bountiful fishing, and excellent snorkeling can be enjoyed in a relatively serene atmosphere.

The island is accessible by ferryboats from two different mainland locations. From the fishing village of Puerto Juárez, five miles north of Cancún, a passenger ferry leaves for Isla Mujeres about every two hours throughout the day. Three miles farther north, at Punta Sam, an auto ferry (which also carries passengers without vehicles), makes the trip on a slightly less frequent basis. Although you can drive around the island, there are few places of any considerable distance to go, and transportation is cheap and abundant; taxi fares are regulated, and bicycles and small motorbikes are available by the hour or the day. So there is no compelling reason to make the trip with an automobile.

At Puerto Juárez, a small information booth where you can obtain information about the next departure is located at the wharf. You might be offered passage on a private boat, but the fare is likely to be seven or eight times the cost of the ferry. On the dock, pushcart vendors sell succulent fruits, such as apples and mangoes peeled and carved into the shapes of flowers. Along the shoreline, donkeys bray in nearby yards and exotic birds screech in the palms.

Photo by Lorie Brillinger

Waiting for the mainland ferry

Like an oversized version of the *African Queen*, the large wooden boat chugs in across the calm waters and ties up to the dock. For a half-hour or so, passengers climb on board and settle onto the wooden benches. On one trip you are likely to hear four or five different languages, perhaps including French, German, and Swedish, as well as Spanish and English, reflecting the diversity of tourists mixed with local commuters. Young Mexican men and women load on large bundles of natively produced hammocks, piñatas, and other handicrafts for sale on the island. Already, as the boat sets off on its 45-minute voyage across the sea, the slightly crazed rush of arriving in Cancún and hustling to Puerto Juárez has subsided, melting into the soothing, warm, and salty breeze.

Isla Mujeres was named by Spanish explorers in 1517.

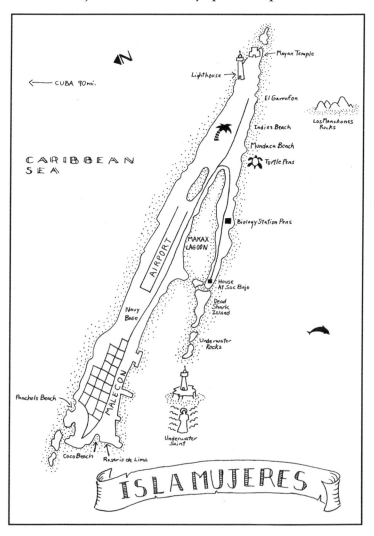

Impressed by the many female icons they found on the island, the conquistadors called it "Island of Women." Today the last remaining vestige of the original Mayan civilization is a small temple ruin at the rocky, southernmost tip. As you approach the island by ferry, however, the evidence of modernism gathers shape on the northwestern shore, where the hotels, restaurants, and tourist shops are crowded together amidst the houses and shops of the island population. Tall palm trees rise up around the densely constructed town, enhancing the exotic image of the island, which is otherwise fairly flat and covered mostly by scrubby jungle.

At the landing the commotion of tourists, taxis, and vendors can be initially intimidating. The taxi stand is located next to the dock, but almost all the restaurants and hotels are within walking distance. During the tourist season (December 15-April 15), it is wise to make reservations in advance. Otherwise, Isla Mujeres offers a full range of accommodations. Several medium-priced hotels, such as the Vistal Mar, and more expensive modern hotels, like the Posada del Mar, are located along the Avenida Rueda Medina, which runs from the pier along the western beachfront. Toward the northern tip of the island, near the snow-white sands of Playa Los Cocos, are the inexpensive, concrete and thatch-roofed bungalows of the Cabañas Zazil-Ha, while farther around the island's tip, past Playa Norte, stands the beautifully located but pretentiously designed, surprisingly nonluxurious, and now-closed 100-room Hotel El Presidente Caribe. Two resort hotels are situated out of town, down the western coast: Maria's, with romantic pink stucco bungalows around a shady palm

The dock at Maria's Kankin Hotel

garden, offers a French-Mexican restaurant with outdoor dining; and Hacienda Gomar, an ambitious complex with shops, hotel rooms, and a large dining room and terrace near the beach.

For the least expensive centrally located hotels, follow one of the narrow streets (Aves. Morelos and Bravo) straight ahead from the pier. In the interior of town, you'll find a variety of small, inexpensive, and moderately priced hotels —the Hotels Martinez, Berny, Osorio, Caracol, and Caribe Maya, for instance—some with air conditioning, others with ceiling fans. On the eastern, rocky side of the island, only a three-block walk, two hotels overlook the rough surf of the ocean: the newer Rocas del Caribe; and the slightly older, more picturesque Hotel Rocamar, perched on a high corner of town right above the town square.

Once settled, you can start your explorations of the

island. The town, just a few blocks wide and only slightly longer, readily becomes familiar. Street names are of little use, but it's virtually impossible to get lost, as you quickly learn such major reference points as the pier, the *zócalo* (town square), the lighthouse tower, and the hotels and restaurants. You begin to recognize the faces around town. The people are smiling and friendly, yet go about their business without undue attention to tourists. Fellow visitors become neighbors and share stories over dinner, then stroll around town in the evening. You become aware of the changes in the light—hard and bright under blue skies, or soft and muted under the cloud cover of a passing tropical storm. And you become conscious of the pervasive, intoxicating scent of mangoes and papayas in the air. Within a day, the warm city and the sultry weather fit as comfortably as a well-worn shirt.

The Avenida Hidalgo is the main central street, running north from the town square. It has been modestly reshaped and landscaped into a narrow mall and, like most of the streets, is well lighted at night. A stroll down Avenida Hidalgo and out along the branching byways is enough for you to get your bearings.

The town offers a great temptation to laze around in the sun on the beaches, browse leisurely through the many shops, stop for a snack and a beer at one of the many *taquerias* and restaurants, or just sit and watch children playing *beisbol* or *futbol* (soccer) on the beach. At Playa Norte, an excellent place to swim at the edge of town, young, athletic travelers play volleyball and stretch out on the sand, taking breaks at the two snack bars on the beach. The streets of the village bustle with activity until siesta, when many businesses close for several hours, especially during the summer. At dusk, the town jumps back to life. A heated basketball game, on the José Del C. Pastrana court in the *zócalo*, usually starts up at sundown, with local teens and young adults teaming up against tourists. Fans gather spontaneously and cheer one side or the other, taking breaks to fetch a fresh milkshake from the corner ice cream stand or a cold drink from the supermarket across the square, next to the movie house.

As night falls, the town begins to shimmer with increased activity under the bright streetlights. People line up at the pushcarts in front of the supermarket to buy fresh fruit. Children play in the streets and in the broad plaza in front of the Teatro del Puebla. A net is strung across the court, and volleyball replaces basketball as the sports attraction. Tourists, relaxed and contented from a hearty dinner, wander slowly through the shops. Occa-sionally a band sets up its equipment and plays popular Caribbean music from the steps of the municipal building.

But the pleasures of Isla Mujeres extend far beyond the town. With the early rise of the tropical sun, a whole different landscape of adventure unfolds. Although it's not out of the question to walk, and while taxis are very cheap, the fun way to explore the island is on motorbike, golf cart, or mountain bike, which can be rented from several locations for less than $10 per day. A short loop around the northern end takes you to Playa Los Cocos—the best swimming beach—where you can rent *tablas del viento* for windsurfing. The two-lane road south along the western shoreline, the Garrafón Highway, leads past the small army base and the Makas Lagoon. The island's other main swimming beach, Playa Lancheros, is just off the road, with shady *palapas* shelters, a snack stand, and wooden pens for sea turtles.

Near Playa Lancheros is the decayed estate of 19th-century slave trader Fermin Mundaca. The pirate built his fortress on Isla Mujeres in the mid-1800s, creating his own paradise of grand buildings and gardens in his quest for the love of a beautiful *mujer* of the island. All that remain of his lush Hacienda de la Huerta (Estate of the Happy Orchard) are shady yet evocative ruins. These will be developed into a park, according to signs at the site.

Farther south is the island's most wondrous natural resource, El Garrafón. Here, the combination of a large coral reef and exceptionally clear, gentle water provides hours

Photo by Lorie Brillinger

Friends on La Playa Norte

of good snorkeling. The beach is set up as a park, with a nominal entry fee, and is geared for heavy tourist traffic, so be sure to come early or late. A restaurant, an aquarium/ museum, hamburger and ice cream stands, clothing and curio shops, and snorkel equipment rental stands are scattered across the terraced hillside. Large numbers of tourists are boated in daily from Cancún. But the crowd thins out in midafternoon, and the snorkeling is spectacular. Hundreds of species of fish of every imaginable color and shape blithely feed on the reef and swim by in enormous schools.

If you can bear to leave El Garrafón, the southern tip of the island is just a half-kilometer away. A path leads past the lighthouse to the small remains of a Mayan temple, dramatically perched on the cliff above the crashing waves. Most people return to town on the same highway, but the road loops around to the eastern coastline, where the shore is rugged and beautiful. The deserted beaches, with their heavier surf and gusty breezes, provide a chance to be alone (away from all the others who are "getting away from it all"), to comb the beach, gather shells and driftwood, and watch the waves.

Any appetite worked up during an adventurous day on Isla Mujeres can be easily satisfied. *Taquerias* and restaurants in every price range abound. Although what is conventionally considered "Mexican food" is available, and some of the enchiladas, *tortas*, and *chilaquiles* are quite good, the main fare of the island is grilled fresh shrimp, fish, and conch, served with lime, rice, and fresh, handmade tortillas. The smaller restaurants, such as Sergio's, the Buccanero, La Mano de Dios, or Giltry, are very inexpensive, with entire meals for $2 or $3. Such larger, fancier

Photo by Margaret Scott

The lighthouse, southern tip of Isla Mujeres

establishments as Gomar, Ciro's, or Maria's, specializing in lobster, shrimp, conch, and turtle, are hardly bargains, but provide fine service and a hint of luxury. For breakfast, the ideal setting can be found at the outdoor restaurants on the beach near the pier, where you can sit under thatched roofs and watch the boats go out.

A day or two is obviously not enough time to savor all the delights of Isla Mujeres. But the island's most attractive characteristic is the freedom it provides visitors—freedom to choose from a variety of activities and adventures, to shape their own days and nights, and to determine their own pace. Somewhere between the overdevelopment of nearby Cancún and the natural state of a desert island, Isla Mujeres waits, a crossroads temporarily suspended in time, with almost any direction possible.

NOTEWORTHY

Snorkeling at El Garrafón: The coral reef, the remarkably clear waters, and the abundance of exotic tropical fish conspire to provide some of the most accessible and intriguing snorkeling in the Caribbean. A nominal admission fee is required for entrance to the park. Equipment rentals are available at the beach. If the area around the main channel looks crowded, enter the water near the long pier to the left. Again, it's best to come either early or late in the day.

Isla Contoy, an uninhabited island north of Isla Mujeres, has a marvelous bird sanctuary. Several entrepreneurs organize an entire day's outing that includes fishing, grilling and eating the catch, and snorkeling, with a long stopover on Contoy to observe the stunning variety of cormorants, pelicans, herons, egrets, and other birds. Scuba diving and deep-sea fishing trips can also be easily arranged.

WHERE TO STAY

Hotel Rocamar
Avenidas Nicolas Bravoy and Guerrero
Isla Mujeres, Quintana Roo, Mexico
Telephone: (011) 52-98-82-01-01
Located on the eastern side of the island at the corner of the town square, the Hotel Rocamar sits right on the edge of the sea. Most of the large rooms have balconies perched virtually on top of the breakers. Although there are signs of weathering and minor disrepair, the Rocamar boasts a certain charm and is one of the island's best deals. The combination of ceiling fans and constant sea breeze keeps the rooms cool, and the roaring song of the surf lulls you to sleep at night. Rates start at about $35 double.

Posada del Mar
Avenida Rueda Marina No. 15
Isla Mujeres, Quintana Roo, Mexico
Telephone: (011) 52-98-87-03-00
Designed for the traveler who wants a bit of luxury without the impersonal nature of the Cancún resorts, the Posada del Mar has 41 rooms and bungalows (with air conditioning or ceiling fans) spread out around its neatly maintained palm gardens and grounds. Facing the western beach, it offers such amenities as a fountain-fed swimming pool, restaurant, and patio bar. Rates start at $35 double in summer, and $60 in winter.

Maria's Kankin
P.O. Box 69
77400 Isla Mujeres, Quintana Roo, Mexico
Telephone: (011) 52-98-83-14-20; fax: (011) 52-98-87-03-95
Perfect for a romantic getaway in the honeymoon spirit, Maria's Kankin is tucked into a lush setting of palms and flowering vegetation. Its pink stucco exterior adds to the charm of the terraced design. The patio bar and restaurant look out over the hotel's private beach and private pier for hotel guests. Rates start at $50 for two.

A mural in Isla town

Hotel Na-Balam
Calle Zazil Ha No. 118
Isla Mujeres, Quintana Roo, Mexico 77400
Telephone: (011) 52-98-77-023-79; fax: (011) 52-98-77-04-46
The spacious one-bedroom suites (refrigerator, ceiling fans)
are a bargain at $55 for two in the summer and $75 in winter. Meals are served in the garden patio (fresh homemade
wheat bread, the best fresh orange juice in the world, and
good coffee). Ask for Bernardo, a great waiter. A slight dis-
advantage of Na-Balam is the shallow water. For deep-water
swimming, you need to walk ten minutes toward town. The
private terrace overlooks the North Beach, the perfect spot
to watch the sunset.

RESTAURANTS

It would take more than a week to eat your way through
Isla Mujeres, so numerous and diverse are the restaurants.
Using your instinct, pocketbook, and best of all, tips from
other travelers, you can make dining another branch of exploration. Sergio's, on the east side of town facing the town
square, is an inexpensive spot for good fried fish. Its patio
dining area is also a good spot to sit in the early evening for
a cold drink and a snack of guacamole and tortilla chips.

The Buccanero, an open air restaurant in the middle
of town, serves excellent enchiladas, very cold soft drinks
and beer, and a variety of local specialties.

Maria's Kankin is romantically situated in a classically
tropical setting out of town on the western coast of the island. The outdoor dining room is nestled in palms and
looks out over the water. Menus are hand-printed on

Photo by Lorie Brillinger

The Grill at El Sombrero del Gomar

woven straw mats. The dishes include local seafood (fresh live lobster a specialty), excellently prepared in Mexican and Continental styles. Although it is one of the more expensive places to eat on Isla Mujeres, it is also one of the loveliest.

El Limbo is the grottolike restaurant nestled under the Hotel Rocamar. Its decor is simple but intriguing, with a seashell motif reflected in the tile floor and walls. Windows overlook the breakers on the eastern coast. The food is very good, with different varieties of fresh seafood prepared in several local styles. Watch out for the salsa; it is fiery.

Brisas del Caribe, a thatch-roofed patio restaurant located a few steps from the ferry dock, is a perfect place for a sunrise breakfast. Fresh orange juice and delicious banana hotcakes are among the offerings.

Ciro's Lobster House is one of the two or three large restaurants in the central section of the village. Although it is tourist oriented, with a fully stocked bar and a television, many of the dishes are excellent. Lobster is the specialty, but the menu is extensive, and the soups are delicious.

Pizza Rolandi has the best pizza in the Americas. Try the shrimp pizza, then finish with coconut ice cream smothered in Kahlua. El Sombrero del Gomar, upstairs, with a second-floor balcony that overlooks a busy intersection, offers great people-watching and good food.

FROM MY JOURNAL

As we pulled our motorbikes up to the gate at the Hacienda Gomar, three young teenaged boys approached, hauling wet burlap gunnysacks. They had just emerged from the lagoon, and their bags were full of shells. One boy pulled out a large conch shell and put its point to his pursed lips and blew. A long, moaning note drifted into the air. The other boys laughed as he handed me the shell and I blew a loud, flatulent rasp from the conch. They set a few of their prizes on the ground before us, and we picked out a beautiful tiger-striped specimen. They parted with it for about $5; it would sell for $12 to $15 in town.

Today there was no one walking along the eastern beaches, where the waves are wild and beautiful. Maybe it was the darkening sky and the smell of rain, which just seemed to make it more romantic. Tonight the ocean went crazy outside our window, making thunder against the rocks below the hotel. We opened our shutters wide to the crashing serenade.

HOW TO GET THERE

From Cancún, travel by taxi or bus to Puerto Juárez and take the passenger ferry to Isla Mujeres. With an automobile, drive to Punta Sam, three miles north of Puerto Juárez, and take the car ferry.

Photo by Derk Richardson

Ferry dock on Isla Mujeres

Isla Holbox

As you ride through the Yucatán jungle toward Chiquila, the mainland harbor nearest Isla Holbox, it's as if layers of civilization and pretense are peeled away before your eyes, preparing you for the simple fishing village island that rests an hour's boat ride across the sea. Along Highway 180, between Mérida and Puerto Juárez, the tourists zoom back and forth, heading to Chichén Itzá and Cancún, oblivious to the remote beauty to the north. But once you make the turn at the junction just west of Nuevo Xcan, the pace slackens and the quiet nature of the villages along the road takes hold.

Isla Holbox lies off the northeastern tip of the Yucatán Peninsula, surrounded by the clear blue Gulf waters. Although it is 15 miles long and two miles across at its widest point, the island is inhabited only at the western end, you'll find the small pueblo of Holbox, with perhaps 100 houses. Its people live by grace of the sea and their own small gardens. Since few tourists ever find their way to Isla Holbox, the island offers a tranquil picture of indigenous life where the Gulf of Mexico meets the

Caribbean, a life unspoiled by the crass commerce of hotels, restaurants, and curio shops. Without the lure of the typical resort-town amenities and tourist attractions, Holbox challenges the visitor to creatively explore the unadorned setting and all its intrinsic beauty.

Much of the adventure is in getting there. Chiquila is within a few hours' drive of Cancún, Cobá, or Valladolid, but direct public buses run on a regular schedule only from Valladolid. They are timed to meet the ferries to Isla Holbox. Access from either the east (Cancún) or the west (Valladolid or Mérida) is via Highway 180 to El Ideal, where one turns north. The paved two-lane road is good, and the sparse traffic moves briskly between the towns on the 46-mile (75-km) stretch from El Ideal to Chiquila. But as each village crops up almost rhythmically along the way, and as the jungle flora gradually change from the dense inland growth to the lighter vegetation nearing the seashore, the scenery grows more absorbing, and you find yourself slowing down to take it all in. Each small town has its variations on the same themes. Around the houses with their thatched *palapa* roofs, lines of brightly colored laundry sway in the breeze—reds, purples, and yellows set off against the dark green tropical foliage. Chickens, hogs, and turkeys amble along the roadside, sometimes crossing your path at their own leisure. Children stare intently as you drive by, their faces sometimes breaking into friendly smiles as they shyly respond to a wave. Every pueblo seems to have a baseball diamond and a basketball court, and such larger ones as Kantunilkin and San Angel have *zócalos*, or town squares.

At the end of the road, Chiquila appears to be little

Photo by Dave Fogerty

Posada Flamingo's welcome sign near ferry dock

more than a few houses and a solitary boat dock with only
the slightest activity between the arrivals and departures of
the ferries. Be open to unforeseen circumstances. On our
first attempt to reach Holbox, we arrived at Chiquila in the
afternoon during an especially blustery storm. The wind
was creating large whitecaps on the sea and blowing the
warm, heavy rain horizontally across the pier. When the ferries arrived from Holbox, the passengers were drenched.
The captain of the auto ferry decided not to chance the return trip. We opted to drive back to Cobá and return in the
morning, rather than brave the turbulent waves on the passenger ferry.

A large scow serves as the car ferry, able to transport
two small cars or a truck, but as there is virtually no driving
to do on Holbox, you can leave your car near the dock and

take the passenger boat, which can carry up to 50 people inside. The captain and his mate tie the boat to the pier and assist the passengers aboard, waiting to collect the fare during the hour-long trip. You ride with the regulars who commute to work or shop on the mainland, and you are unlikely to encounter any non-Spanish-speaking travelers. The ride is slow, rolling, and as smooth as the weather will allow. If a storm whips up, bringing the sea to a froth, the boat rocks and dips like a roller coaster. But on a calm day, the trip is easy and comfortable. As Isla Holbox comes into view, you may notice a bold swatch of pink in a lagoon off to the left. As the boat draws closer, a sudden commotion erupts and the patch of bright pink starts to scatter and rise, as the large flock of flamingos takes flight. Launching their gangly bodies into graceful motion, the exotic birds soar in great circles and land in the shallow water once the boat has passed. It's just the first glimpse of Holbox's simple but elegant natural wonders.

Where the ferry docks, a dirt road leads from the pier into the village. If you arrive in midmorning, with the sun already high in the sky, the pueblo may look parched and desolate. A baseball diamond sits in disrepair off to the right. Only a few people are visible on the dusty streets, and the disembarking passengers seem to vanish mysteriously on the trek into town. But the hidden life and appeal of Holbox gradually unfold as you leave the pier.

Just 40 yards or so from the dock, past the town's power plant, stands one of the town's four restaurants, the El Paso—a screened, circular patio with a palm roof. Two others are farther along the same road, closer to the town's main square, where the local government offices, post office, and telegraph station are located. The town is comprised of only five to ten square blocks of houses, and as you walk through, you will catch glimpses of women preparing meals and doing laundry and children playing games in the small yards. Among the first things to catch your eye along the street near every house are great piles of large conch and other shells, discarded casually after the fish has been removed.

If you walk straight ahead on the road from the pier, you come quickly to the other side of the island, where the fishing boats are tied up, and where a breathtaking expanse of white beach extends for a mile to the west and two miles to the east. Large pelicans and other seabirds amble along the shore or swoop overhead. Here, along the open sea and its surprisingly gentle, clear blue waters, is the chief

Photo by Dave Fogerty

Local fishing boats at a gulf-side beach

allure of Holbox for the adventurous visitor—a beach-comber's paradise. Just a few minutes' walk down the beach takes you away from the village to where there is nothing but shallow ocean to one side and the tangled scrub of jungle to the other.

The sand is littered with millions of shells of every variety. In some places they cover the beach completely, crunching under foot as you walk along. There is perhaps no greater abundance of whelks, cockles, bubbles, lion's paws, and other shells anywhere else along the Yucatán Peninsula. The first sight of all those treasures is overwhelming, and as you walk along the shore, the realization sinks in that they are just a tiny representation of the rich and varied life in the surrounding sea. And except for a fishing boat or two, you may come across no other signs of life. At many points along the deserted beach, you can wade out a great distance into the water and cool your feet or swim.

If you arrive at Holbox in the morning, you can get in two or three hours of relaxed beachcombing before walking back to the village. The activity picks up as families prepare for their midday meals, frying the day's catch, pounding cornmeal into tortillas, and cooking up pots of beans and rice. After several hours of beachcombing, we walked back through town and encountered the ferryboat skipper on his stopover between runs. He commented on the conch shells we had picked up, reminded us of the departure time, and directed us to the restaurant near the pier. At the El Paso, the fare is determined by what the sea has yielded to the fishermen that day. Generous portions of fish are deliciously grilled, served with a stack of fresh, warm, homemade corn tortillas. Black beans are served in a flavorful broth, with sliced hot peppers on the side. Add a cold bottle of beer, soda, or mineral water, and you could not ask for a heartier, more satisfying meal for the price (about $2).

Isla Holbox can be enjoyed for the day without much more than the few words of Spanish needed to order a meal and ask directions. A fluent command of the language will allow you greater access to the life of the island. Be sure to check the departure time of the ferry returning to Chiquila. However long you stay, the subtle magic of this remote island lingers well after you've watched it slowly vanish behind you, as the ferry takes you back to the Yucatán mainland.

Photo by Dave Fogery

Main Street, sleepy Holbox town

WHERE TO STAY

Hotel Flamingo

Holbox, Q. Roo, CP 77310, Mexico
Telephone: (011) 52-918-872-983, Ext. 102
A good place to stay is the Hotel Flamingo, close to the ferry dock. This offers five clean, simple rooms, each with bathroom and shower, fan, and mosquito nets for about $10 per night ($12 high season). It is operated by Señor Garcia, formerly the "Captain of the Port," the most important Mexican official on the island, who is in charge of the ferries and docks. Señor Garcia is a good source for information about Holbox and can arrange boat excursions.

Hotel Ingrid

Holbox, Q. Roo, CP 77310, Mexico
Six new rooms, each with private bath, opened in 1994 on the Caribbean side of the island.

RESTAURANTS

El Paso, near the pier, grills fish to perfection. The warm homemade corn tortillas and black beans make an inexpensive, memorable meal. Sarabanda, Miguel Angel, and Restaurante del Parque also serve good local food.

HOW TO GET THERE

Take a car or bus to the village of Chiquila, 46 miles (75 km) north from Highway 180 at El Ideal. Direct buses run several times a day to and from Valladolid, timed to connect with the ferries. There is no direct bus to Chiquila from

Cancún, but an enterprising traveler who speaks a little Spanish can take a bus from Cancún and ask the driver to be dropped off at El Ideal. From there one can either wait to catch a bus from Valladolid bound for Chiquila, or negotiate a taxi ride from El Ideal to Chiquila. There are nearly always several taxis waiting at the El Ideal junction. When I did this, it cost me about $15, with the taxi driver picking up other passengers along the way to lower the fare. The ferry leaves Chiquila for Isla Holbox three times a day, at 8:00 a.m., 11:30 a.m., and 3:30 p.m., weather permitting, and makes the trip from Holbox at 6:30 a.m., 10:00 a.m., and 2:00 p.m. A private boat is 240 Mexican pesos (U.S. $40) round trip.

PRACTICAL TIPS

Immigration: Proof of U.S. citizenship and a tourist card (provided free of charge by your travel agent or airline) are required for entry to Mexico. Save the carbon copy of your tourist card to present on departure. You'll need 72 Mexican pesos (U.S. $12) for the departure tax.

Currency: The Mexican peso fluctuates daily, but was approximately six to U.S. $1 at publication time.

Language: Spanish is the local language, and you'll hear little else on Holbox. Some English is spoken on Isla Mujeres.

Health: Avoid tap water. Mineral water is excellent and inexpensive.

CAYMAN ISLANDS

The Cayman Islands, 480 miles south of Miami, are a British Crown Colony—a friendly mix of English, Irish, Welsh, Scottish, and African. Grand Cayman, the largest, is a bustling tourist center with the highest standard of living in the Caribbean. Sister islands Little Cayman and Cayman Brac, 30 minutes away by twin-propeller plane, have changed little since Christopher Columbus first saw them in 1503. Both of these small, flat islands are actually pinnacles rising 5,000 feet from the ocean floor. In the crystal-clear water that surrounds them is some of the best scuba diving to be found anywhere in the Northern Hemisphere: cavern dives, wreck dives, wall dives, and exploration dives.

Little Cayman

L ittle Cayman is the way it was and still is," says native Sam McCoy. It would be hard to imagine an island any quieter, for there are just two dozen permanent residents. More than 90 percent of the island remains uninhabited and undeveloped—the airport is a grass landing strip, while most of the roads are unpaved trails. Quiet paths lead into the jungle bush, alive with wildlife and birds including boobies, iguanas, and parrots. A great salt pond is filled with a miniature version of tarpon.

The spectacular vertical walls and living coral reefs of Little Cayman are legendary among experienced divers. The sea is so clear, with no mountain runoff or pollution, that visibility averages between 125 and 200 feet year-round. That combined with the extended reefs and abundant marine life provide ultimate diving and snorkeling for the traveler seeking a quiet, unspoiled island retreat.

NOTEWORTHY

Bloody Bay Marine Park: A dive beneath the ocean's mirror-smooth surface into Bloody Bay Marine Park is a voyage into the third dimension, a world of lush coral gardens, giant sponges, trees of black coral, elaborate sea fans, and majestic eagle rays. The park teems with life: yellowtails, sergeant majors, angelfish, green morays, tarpons, octopuses, and silversides, as well as semi-tame grouper, jewfish, and eels that allow close inspection. At one place along Bloody Bay Wall, the drop-off begins in 18 feet of water and plummets vertically to 1,200 feet. This may be the most beautiful dive spot in the Caribbean!

Spear guns are prohibited, and no type of marine life of any kind can be taken from the park. Access is limited, and only dive operations licensed by the Marine Conservation Board may bring divers.

Spring through fall is the best time for diving here.

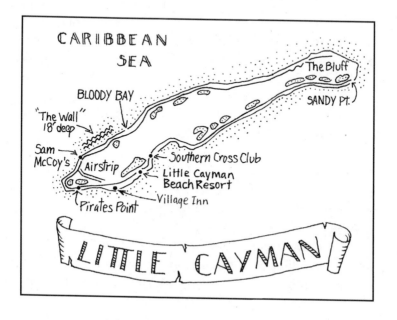

During the winter, strong prevailing northeasterlies mean that glassy-smooth seas are uncommon, although underwater visibility remains good in all seasons.

Governor Gore Bird Sanctuary: Located off Guy Banks Road along the southeastern coastline, the bird sanctuary is home to 5,000 pairs of red-footed boobies and about 100 pairs of magnificent frigate birds.

WHERE TO STAY

Pirates Point Resort

Little Cayman, British West Indies
Telephone: (809) 948-4610; fax: (809) 948-4611
Gladys Howard is owner-manager of this ten-room diving resort located on five beachfront acres. An avid diver and *cordon bleu* chef, Gladys provides a friendly, hospitable second home for her guests. "My guests set their own schedules for diving and fishing," she says, "and the kitchen never closes." In summer, rates are $220 single and $360 per couple; $220 and $360 in winter. Rates include all meals, wine, trips to reefs, tanks and diving equipment, bicycles, and transportation to the airport. There are lower "just relaxing" rates for non-divers.

Southern Cross Club

Little Cayman, British West Indies
Telephone: U.S. telephone: (800) 899-2582;
fax: (317) 636-9503
There are five duplex bungalows at this casual beachfront hotel. Everything is run family style; no room keys exist (crime is unknown on the island), and you can prepare

your own drinks at the honor bar. Bicycles and windsurfing equipment are provided, and a dive master is there to rent equipment and arrange trips to the reefs. In summer, rates run $105 single, $180 per couple, including three meals.

The Village Inn
Blossom Village, Little Cayman
British West Indies
Telephone: (809) 949-1069; fax: (809) 948-0069
Newly built since our last visit, each of the seven units includes a fully equipped kitchen.

"Your stay will not be interrupted by the blare of television, ringing of telephones, or monotone alarm clocks," says owner Dave Tibbetts, "because we have none of them." Units go for $110 single, $125 double, with lower rates in the summer.

Sam McCoy's Fishing and Diving Lodge
P.O. Box 1725
Little Cayman, British West Indies
Telephone: (809) 949-2891; fax: (809) 949-6821;
U.S. telephone: (800) 626-0496
This Caymanian family-owned and -operated diving lodge has eight double rooms. Daily rates are $117 per person ("relax") and $159 ("dive"). Both include three native-style meals. Parent alert: babysitting service is available!

Little Cayman Beach Resort
Blossom Village
Little Cayman, British West Indies
Telephone: (809) 948-4533; fax: (809) 948-4533;
U.S. telephone: (800) 327-3835
The spacious beachfront rooms (all are disabled accessible) go for $119 single and $129 double. Tennis, pool, and a full scuba center are part of the scene.

RESTAURANTS

The only food on Little Cayman is served at your guest house or hotel.

HOW TO GET THERE

Island Air operates flights daily from Grand Cayman and Cayman Brac. Flying time is approximately 30 minutes. U.S. telephone (800) 922-9626 for current flight schedules and reservations.

Cayman Brac

As the twin-propeller plane lands from thriving Grand Cayman, Cayman Brac greets you with an overwhelming first impression: sunlight bouncing off the white sand through crystal-clear aquamarine water.

Twelve miles long and an average of 1.5 miles wide, the island has 1,300 residents, most of whom live along the north coast, where the island's distinctive old Brac houses, schools, church, and museum are located. The south coast is a virtually unchanged natural landscape, home to scores of bird and plant species.

The most striking feature on the island is the bluff (*brac* in Gaelic), a formidable geologic formation riddled with more than 100 caves, including Rebekah's Cave, Bat's Cave, Great Cave, and Cliff Cave. Steps have been carved in the side of the brac at a point in Spot Bay, and the walk to the plateau at the top is well worth the effort for the views along the way. Boobies with long pointed wings whirl and swoop from the bluff to the sea and back.

The bluff yields veins of caymanite, a semi-precious gemstone found only in the Cayman Islands. It is

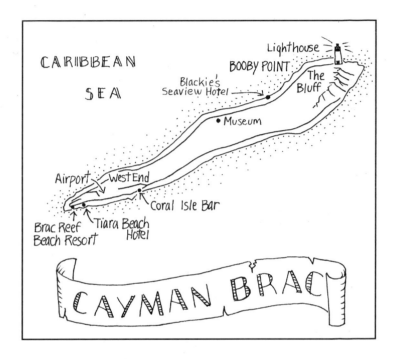

a protected natural resource, and only two islanders are licensed to extract it. The color streaks dictate the form as pieces are cut and polished for distinctive jewelry.

Cayman Brac has superb shore diving as well as boat diving; there are more than 40 excellent dive sites, with additional ones being discovered every year. The majority of them are at the western end of the island, making the boat rides from the two dive resorts quick and convenient. Both sides of the Brac offer excellent diving, including awesome drop-offs, unique underwater attractions, and high-quality, shallow/medium-depth coral gardens.

NOTEWORTHY

The Hobbit is a drop-off less than a quarter-mile east of the Tiara Beach Resort. Named after the classic by J.R.R. Tolkien, the drop-off has a fairyland appearance that features a number of giant, bizarre-looking sponges. Fish life here is extremely active and includes blue runner jacks, barracudas, and ocean triggerfish.

The Cayman Brac Museum: Historical artifacts, including pirate treasure and pictures of some of the major hurricanes to strike the island, are among the items to see at this Stake Bay museum.

WHERE TO STAY

Divi Tiara Beach Hotel
Cayman Brac, British West Indies
Telephone: (809) 948-7553; fax: (809) 948-7316;
U.S. telephone: (800) 367-3484
This modern beachfront resort is considered the largest and most successful dedicated dive resort in the Cayman Islands. Rooms are air-conditioned but also have ceiling fans. There are tennis courts, a swimming pool, and diving and windsurfing equipment; underwater photo classes are also available. In summer, single rooms start at $95, $120 per couple, increasing to $125 for one or two in winter.

Brac Reef Beach Resort

P.O. Box 235, West End
Cayman Brac, British West Indies
Telephone: (809) 948-7323; U.S. telephone. (800) 327-3835;
U.S. fax: (800) 948-7207

Less than 150 yards east of Divi Tiara, the Brac Reef Beach Resort is another dedicated diving resort with 40 comfortable, modern rooms facing the beach and a breezy, two-story gazebo bar at the end of a jetty. A freshwater pool and Jacuzzi face the long stretch of white sand that slopes toward the sea. Rates start at $89 single, $99 per couple in low season (after April 19); $110 single and $120 per couple for winter. Meal and dive packages are available. Adjacent to the hotel is the headquarters of Brac Aquatics, the Brac's oldest and best-known dive operation.

Brac Caribbean Beach Village

P.O. Box 4, Stake Bay
Cayman Brac, British West Indies
Telephone: (809) 948-2265; fax: (809) 948-2206

This oceanfront condominium hotel has 25 units, each with two bedrooms, two baths, and a fully equipped kitchen. French doors open to a shady veranda, steps from the reef-protected, white sand beach. Year-round rates are $150 daily for one or two persons and $900 weekly.

Blackie's Seaview Hotel
Watering Place
Cayman Brac, British West Indies
Telephone: (809) 948-0232
Each of the nine budget, oceanview rooms has air conditioning and ceiling fans. Within walking distance you'll find a pool, bar, restaurant, and excellent snorkeling. Be sure to try the island's best homemade ice cream.

Apartment Rentals
Trevor Foster
P.O. Box 57, Stake Bay,
Cayman Brac, British West Indies
Telephone: (809) 948-7382

RESTAURANTS

There are a variety of restaurants, including Blackies, off South Side; La Esperanza, at Creek; Ed's Place, at West End; Suahil, at Spot Bay; and Watering Place, at Watering Place.

HOW TO GET THERE

Cayman Airways has nonstop service from Houston, Miami, and Tampa to Grand Cayman. Flying time is just one hour. Cayman Airways has a twin-propeller commuter aircraft that flies from Grand Caymon daily, except on Monday and Tuesday. U.S. telephone (800) 922-9629 for current schedules.

CAYMAN ISLANDS

PRACTICAL TIPS

Immigration: A passport or other proof of U.S. citizenship and a return or ongoing ticket are needed for entrance to the Cayman Islands. The departure tax is $7.50.

Currency: The local currency is the Cayman dollar, with a fixed exchange rate at CI$1 = U.S.$1.20. (However, restaurants and shops will convert at U.S.$1.25 to cover bank charges.)

Reconfirmation: Once you have landed in the Caymans, it is extremely important to reconfirm your return reservations 72 hours (three days) in advance. This is easiest to do on arrival, while the airport is open.

Drugs: The Cayman Islands have the severest anti-drug (marijuana included) laws in the Caribbean. Violators are immediately arrested and taken off to jail.

BRITISH VIRGIN ISLANDS

We found some of the most beautiful islands in the Caribbean in the British Virgin Islands: the finest white sand beaches, the most luminescent sea, excellent snorkeling, friendly English-speaking inhabitants, and thoughtful controls on development.

Unlike the American Virgin Islands, just a few miles to the south, the BVIs (as they are most often called) have no casinos, no slick condominiums, no cruise ships with thousands of passengers docking regularly. Even the largest and most populated BVI has yet to install a traffic light. Life moves quietly and gently in these beautiful islands.

Most of the 51 British Virgin Islands are small and uninhabited, a veritable sailor's paradise of quiet bays, beaches, and goat trails for hiking. Two of the largest BVIs, Tortola and Virgin Gorda, are too well-visited by smart travelers to be called undiscovered. Tortola, the largest island (attached to Beef Island by a bridge), is known for its long, uncrowded beaches, fine local restaurants, and warm hospitality. There are no high-rises on Tortola, no traffic jams, and no frantic pace.

Virgin Gorda is famous for its three outstanding luxury resorts—Little Dix Bay, Biras Creek, and Bitter End—and for its travel-poster-familiar rock formations that provide pools for swimming and snorkeling. We preferred the Olde Yard Inn for its cuisine and good library; and the eight-room, two-villa Drake's Anchorage for its secluded location on tiny (125 acres), privately owned Mosquito Island, 100 yards off mainland Virgin Gorda.

After visiting all of the inhabited BVIs, three stand out as unique and undiscovered: Anegada, Jost Van Dyke, and Guana.

Photo by Burl Willes

Typical British Virgin Islands beach

Anegada

The 15-minute flight in an eight-seater plane from Beef Island (Tortola) passes over no other island; you arrive on this large, flat island feeling you've reached the edge of the world. Goats graze contentedly near the runway, and it is immediately apparent that the island is mostly untrammeled open land. The 12-mile north shore is almost one unbroken stretch of shimmering white sand surrounded by coral reef. With an island population of 290 and a maximum visitor capacity of 36 (hardly ever attained), we calculated that even if everyone went to the beach at the same time, it would still look deserted.

Conch fishing and boat building are the main occupations for the islanders. At The Settlement, which is almost too small and dispersed to be called a town, there are piles of white conch shells just offshore where the fishing boats tie up. The Presbyterian church and the cricket field (teams from other islands come occasionally) are the focal points of island life. If you are here on Sunday, it is well worth visiting the church to hear the fine voices and meet local inhabitants as they come to greet their fellow island neighbors.

Anegada is an island for beach lovers, those who enjoy walking endlessly along a deserted beach, snorkeling in a quiet sea, and swimming in water that is warm and translucent. It is an island for hikers who like tranquil walks far from the noise and pollution of automobiles and motorbikes, and for readers, who will rejoice in the peace, solitude, and unhurried existence of an island lost in time.

NOTEWORTHY

The Anegada Reef has claimed over 300 ships since the age of exploration and is now a diver's paradise. Fish life is abundant, and the wreckage of vessels is easily seen. Within the wreck of *The Rochus,* an incredible array of fish life can be seen.

The rare roseate flamingo, reintroduced from Guana Island, can be seen at the salt ponds.

WHERE TO STAY

Anegada Reef Hotel
Anegada, British Virgin Islands
Telephone: (809) 495-8002; fax: (809) 495-9362
Anegada Reef Hotel is the only place to rent a room on the island. The 16 rooms have recently been improved with small, trellised verandas; air conditioning; private baths; and hot water. Wall-to-wall carpeting and other non-Caribbean furnishings seem intended to reassure visitors that they are safely in the hands of a "civilized" establishment. At the open-air dining room and bar, visitors can enjoy the local specialties, including lobster and conch, while watching

the horizon for sailboats, which regularly drop anchor for lunch and dinner. The white sand beach extends for miles in each direction. Rates, including meals, are $90 per person in summer and $110 in winter. Package dive tours and introductory scuba lessons are available. The hotel owns a fully equipped, 31-foot Bertram for deep-sea fishing.

Neptune's Treasure Campground
The Settlement, Anegada, British Virgin Islands
Telephone: (809) 495-9439
Neptune's Treasure, a five-minute walk along the beach from Anegada Reef Hotel, is an excellent restaurant that serves breakfast, lunch, and dinner to people who moor their boats offshore. They will provide 8' x 10' and 10' x 12' tents and allow you to use the restaurant toilet, which has an outdoor hose for showering. If you bring your own tent, there is a nominal charge for use of the site.

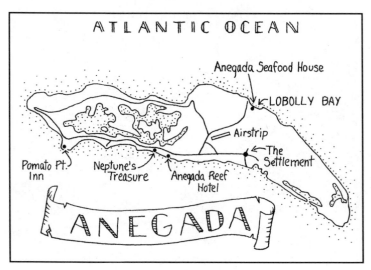

RESTAURANTS

Del's Restaurant and Bar in The Settlement is a full-service restaurant that serves West Indian food daily for breakfast, lunch, and dinner.

At Anegada Seafood House in Loblolly Bay, Diane and Aubrey (he is a native BVIslander, she is from Trinidad) serve delicious food in their open-air restaurant that faces a stretch of white sand. Be sure to try their conch stew.

Neptune's Treasure is run by the friendly Soares family, who came from Bermuda as commercial fishermen more than 20 years ago. Neptune's provides the island's freshest fish and lobster. You can order items from the menu ($12-$25) or what they call "home cooking," which costs a lot less and usually includes fresh fish, vegetables, and salad. Open seven days a week.

Photo by Vincent L. Costa

Anegada-bound plane departs from Beef Island-Tortola

Pomoato Point Beach Restaurant, overlooking a spectacular beach, offers a relaxed and comfortable atmosphere, but alas, is not always open. For lunch and dinner the restaurant serves local dishes of conch, barbecued lobster, and other native seafoods.

HOW TO GET THERE

Gordo Aero flies from Beef Island-Tortola on Monday, Wednesday, Friday, and Sunday. Telephone (809) 495-2271 for current schedules and reservations. Fly BVI provides charter service from Tortola. Telephone (809) 495-2271.

Jost Van Dyke

Jost (rhymes with toast) Van Dyke is a mere 20-minute ferry ride from Tortola's West End, yet the island remains a tranquil setting for anyone seeking a stress-free vacation without automobiles in a setting of exquisite beauty. There are approximately 300 very gracious and hospitable inhabitants.

Arrival from Tortola is at Great Harbour. Verdant hills with flamboyant trees cascade gently down to one of the most perfect beaches we've seen in the Caribbean. Offshore, yachts anchor in clear turquoise water. Two restaurant/bars, a bakery stand, and a small hotel welcome visitors with all the comforts and provisions necessary to make this island the ultimate undiscovered getaway.

To explore the island, there are only two choices: by foot or by boat. The walk over the hill from Great Harbour to White Bay is not long, and the views are breathtaking. The beach at White Bay is perfection. Along the stretch of fine, white sand there are only two houses and a four-cottage hotel. As we swam in the calm, limpid water, a dozen pelicans were our only companions. The local

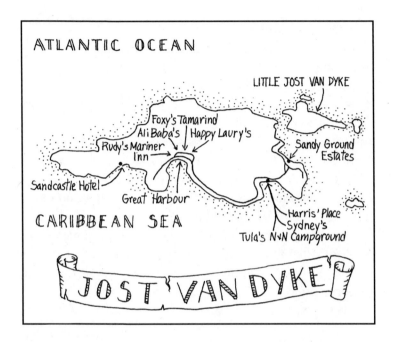

inhabitants are happy to arrange a boat for the return trip or for further exploration to Little Harbour.

WHERE TO STAY

Rudy's Mariner Inn

Great Harbour, Jost Van Dyke, British Virgin Islands
Telephone: (809) 495-9282
Rudy's three-room hotel has kitchenettes, a beach bar and restaurant, a dining patio, and a grocery store. It is very convenient to the ferry landing and nearby nature trails. Rates start at $75 in summer and $95 in the winter.

Sandcastle Hotel
White Bay, Jost Van Dyke, British Virgin Islands
Telephone: (809) 775-5262; fax: (809) 775-3590;
U.S. telephone: (803) 237-8999
This hotel's four cottages are located on one of the most beautiful beaches in the Caribbean. Comfortable and tasteful appointments give an air of luxury, but all lighting is generated by propane lanterns, and showers are outdoors. The restaurant serves gourmet cuisine. (The Culinary Institute of America holds a five-day course in island cooking at the hotel.) Windsurfing, snorkeling equipment, and a Day Sailer are available. Rates, including three meals, are $235 per day for two in off-season, and $295 per day in winter. Be sure to inquire about the cruise ships that now disgorge hundreds of passengers on their beach. Presently this is every third Wednesday and every Friday.

Sandy Ground Estates
P.O. Box 594
West End, Tortola, British Virgin Islands
Telephone: (809) 494-3391
Sandy Ground Estates has eight separate, secluded villas with fully equipped kitchens, each located a short walk from the 800-foot-long private beach. Summer rates are $750 per week; winter, $950.

Harris' Place
Little Harbour, Jost Van Dyke, British Virgin Islands
Telephone: (809) 774-0774
Harris has two basic rooms to rent for $45 to $55 in sum-

mer, and $50 to $65 in winter. There is live reggae music Tuesday and Thursday.

Tula's Enchanted Garden
Little Harbour, Jost Van Dyke, British Virgin Islands
Mailing address: General Delivery, West End, Tortola
British West Indies
Telephone: (809) 495-9566 or 775-3073
Tula's is on the water's edge; a grocery, restaurant, and snack bar are conveniently nearby. This pleasant campsite charges $25 to $35 for 8' x 10' and 9' x 12' tents, $15 for a tent site.

Great Harbour

Photo by Vincent L. Costa

White Bay Campground

White Bay, Jost Van Dyke, British West Indies
Telephone: (809)495-9312
Located on beautiful White Bay, tents are fully furnished with carpet, beds, linen, pots, pans, and lantern. They rent for $20-35; bare sites are $7-10.

RESTAURANTS

Sydney's: This beach bar and restaurant in Little Harbour serves fresh boiled lobster, fish, conch, spareribs, and chicken for lunch or dinner. There is a pig roast every Monday and Saturday night in season.

Ali Baba's, in Great Harbour, is run by Baba Hatchett. The cuisine is West Indian, the drinks are tropical (including Baba's special rum punch), and the atmosphere is casual and friendly. Located west of the customs house, Ali Baba's is open for breakfast, lunch, and dinner. (Make your dinner reservations by 6:00 p.m.)

Foxy's Tamarind, in Great Harbour, serves "family style" dinner six nights a week. Specialties include Rummy Raisin Chicken and grilled local fish. Reservations are requested before 5:00 p.m. Ask about the live calypso music night.

Happy Laury's, located near the main dock on the beach at Great Harbour, specializes in conch fritters, fish, chicken, and chips. The bar is known for a local house drink special, "The Happy Laury Pain Killer," and there is occasional live music by Reuben Chinnery and the Roots.

Harris' Place is located on the water's edge at Little Harbour and is open seven days a week for breakfast, lunch, and dinner. Harris offers a no-wait lunch program. Menu includes lobster, fish, chicken, conch, hamburgers, sandwiches, conch fritters, and other West Indian dishes.

Rudy's Mariner's Rendezvous, tucked into the western end of Great Harbour, specializes in lobster and local fish. Rudy's is open for dinner until 1:00 a.m. Make reservations in person at the customs office.

Sandcastle White Bay offers romantic candlelight dining on a beautiful white sand beach. Lunch is served at 1:30 p.m., and dinner at 7:30 p.m. Dinner entrees include rack of lamb, duck *à l'orange*, and stuffed grouper. Dress is informal; reservations are required.

HOW TO GET THERE

There is no plane service. Jost Van Dyke Ferry Service (telephone 494-2997) operates four times daily between West End, Tortola and Jost Van Dyke, except on Sunday, when there are three crossings. The trip takes 20 minutes and costs $11 round trip.

PRACTICAL TIP

We thank our readers who wrote to say that nights at Great Harbour can be noisy. People flock ashore from visiting yachts, and loud music and voices from the local clubs can reverberate until 2:00 a.m. Bring earplugs if you want to sleep, or stay at one of the island's more remote spots.

Guana Island

Although Guana Island is completely owned by the Guana Island Club, it is so unspoiled and of such interest to nature lovers that we've included it as one of our favorite BVIs. The approach to Guana's dock gives the first hint of the island's 850-acre privacy; there's not a sign of civilization, only a verdant island alive with exotic birds. The island's name comes from the rock formation on the point which looks like the head of an iguana.

Ardent conservationists Gloria and Henry Jarecki purchased the island in 1975 and limit guests to a maximum of 30 at any one time. No homes or condominiums are allowed. There are no other man-made structures beyond the small lodge set on a breeze-swept hill. Guana is a wildlife sanctuary, where lucky zoologists and botanists come to study the native flora and fauna. Rare roseate flamingos, until recently the only ones living in the BVIs, have been reintroduced into the pond. (A gift of 30 were given to Anegada, where they are thriving and multiplying.) Black-necked stilts, herons, egrets, the endangered masked booby, frigate birds, and the rare bridled quail dove are

Photo by Vincent L. Costa

View of White Bay with Tortola in the distance

but a few of the more than 50 species of birds that can be regularly observed on the island.

The miles of nature and walking trails around the island are lined with orchids, jasmine, frangipani, flamboyant, plumeria, oleander, and hibiscus, as well as agave and other native succulents. In the orchard, fresh fruit is picked daily from trees of papaya, mango, orange, grapefruit, lemon, lime, banana, avocado, pineapple, and breadfruit.

There are seven deserted beaches, some for sunning and swimming, some for snorkeling, and two so remote you can reach them only boat. Beneath the pristine surface of the water are 125 species of colorful reef fish.

Guana Island Club
Box 32
Road Town, Tortola, British Virgin Islands
Telephone: (809) 494-2354; U.S. fax (914) 967-8048
These native whitewashed stone cottages were built on
the historic ruins of a centuries-old Quaker estate, which
was once a sugarcane plantation. The 15 rooms are charming and comfortable. Meals in the central clubhouse feature
home-baked breads, island-grown fruits and vegetables, and

complimentary wine. Tennis, croquet, sailing, windsurfing, deep-sea fishing, sunset cruises, and castaway picnics are available. Rates start at $325 per couple in off-season, $595 in peak winter season, and include all meals and all on-island activities. The island's beaches and trails are limited to guests only.

For the ultimate in beachfront seclusion, request North Beach Cottage. This one-bedroom beach house has its own living room, kitchen, sundecks, and rock sea pool. Your only neighbors are sea turtles.

HOW TO GET THERE

Guana's boatmen will meet you at Beef Island (Tortola) Airport for the ten-minute ride.

PRACTICAL TIPS

Immigration: Visitors are welcome in the British Virgin Islands, provided they possess return (or ongoing) tickets. A passport is the principal requirement for entry into the BVIs. For U.S. and Canadian citizens, an authenticated birth certificate or voter registration card, along with photo identification, will suffice. There is an $8 departure tax when leaving by air, $5 by sea.

Currency: BVI currency is the U.S. dollar.

Language: British English with a friendly West Indian accent.

THE BAY ISLANDS OF HONDURAS

About 30 miles offshore from mainland Honduras lies a chain of islands that, until recently, were known only to more adventurous scuba divers. These divers guarded their secret jealously, afraid that once word got out, hordes of tourists would descend on their island paradise, crowding onto the miles of white beaches and invading the pristine reefs with snorkels and fins.

Well, the secret isn't so secret any more. International flights now land at Roatán's tiny airport, a spanking new terminal is slated to open later this year, and eventually the runway will be lighted to allow planes to land at night. International singing star Julio Iglesias was on Roatán when we visited, and rumor had it that he was trying to buy one of the smaller nearby islands. The increase in tourism to mainland Honduras also means more visitors to the islands.

But even though tourism is growing, the hordes have so far failed to descend. Bay Islanders, determined to preserve both the natural riches and the relaxed character of their island home, are controlling the kind and size of development allowed. That means no high-rises, no huge shopping centers, and only one paved road. There are more comfortable accommodations for visitors, but no masses of suntanned bodies thronging the beaches and no discos packed with revelers—just a largely unspoiled tropical paradise with spectacular coral reefs.

Despite the relative ease with which you can now get to the islands, most of the people who come here still come for one reason only: the reefs. Part of one of the largest barrier reefs in the world, extending down from Belize, the Bay Islands' reefs have a well-deserved reputation for world class scuba diving and snorkeling. The quantity and diversity of marine life is impressive by any standards, the water is warm, and, when conditions are right, visibility is excellent. Special attractions for divers include many sheer drop-offs for wall diving, caves, holes, and shipwrecks. Many of the reefs are an easy swim from shore, to the delight of snorkelers and divers alike. In addition to all this, it's cheaper to dive on the Bay Islands than anywhere else in the Caribbean.

Remarkably, the fragile reef environment still seems pristine, despite the inevitable pressures from growth and tourism. Many of the reefs are now protected in marine reserves, and dive operators stress responsible diving practices. Islanders realize that the reefs are their most precious resource, and organizations like the Bay Islands Conservation Association (BICA) work with residents to protect the environment.

In addition to their natural wonders, the Bay Islands have a colorful history and a rich cultural mix. The islands' first inhabitants were the Paya Indians, relatives of the

Maya. Sixteenth-century Spanish explorers and traders carried off Payans to use as slave labor, and later exiled many to the mainland. Today the only reminders of the Payan inhabitants are the many artifacts that still turn up at archaeological sites around the islands.

The Spanish used the Bay Islands to provision their ships, but established no permanent settlements there. In the 16th and 17th centuries, English, Dutch, and French pirates holed up on the islands between their raids on gold-bearing ships from the New World. Henry Morgan, John Coxen, and Ned Lowe are just a few of the famous and much-feared buccaneers who stocked their ships here, and stories are inevitably told of buried treasure still waiting to be dug up.

English settlers first arrived in the 1630s, but were driven off by the Spanish. England and Spain vied for control of the islands for much of the 18th century, and in 1742, the British military occupied Roatán, building fortifications at Port Royal. They vacated in 1752 after signing a treaty with Spain. The first permanent settlement on the islands, at Punta Gorda on Roatán, was established in 1797 by Garifuna (or Black Carib) people. The Garifuna, descendants of Island Carib Indians and African slaves, were forcibly relocated from the island of St. Vincent after rebelling against British rule there. Garifuna people today live on the Honduras coast and on some of the smaller cays of the Bay Islands, as well as at Punta Gorda.

White and black Cayman Islanders emigrated to the Bay Islands in the 1830s, establishing many of the settlements found there today. Great Britain annexed the Bay Islands as a colony in 1852, but pressure from the United

States helped force the English to cede the islands to Honduras in 1859.

Island culture remains quite distinct from that of mainland Honduras, and there are residents who will readily tell you they would prefer British rule. But recent waves of immigrants from the mainland in search of work in the fishing or tourism industries have created closer ties between the islands and the rest of Honduras. Although it's difficult to get accurate figures on the islands' current population, Roatán is believed to have about 30,000 inhabitants, some 20,000 of whom have come from the mainland in the last ten years. Spanish is becoming as common as English in some places (more so on Guanaja), and many people are bilingual. There are also a number of expatriates from Europe and North America who have settled here. In general, islanders seem to get along quite well, regardless of their backgrounds.

Change may be coming to the Bay Islands, but if the residents have their way, it won't touch the friendly and relaxing atmosphere. Here you can forget about clocks and schedules, and crime is practically nonexistent (unless you count the prices some cab drivers on Roatán try to charge). After a few days in the Bay Islands, you'll find it easy to understand why some of those who came in search of an island getaway decided to make this their home.

Roatán

Most visitors to the Bay Islands will never go further than Roatán, and for good reason. At 49 square miles, it is the largest and most diverse of the islands, and also has the most amenities for travelers. The extensive reef system surrounding it teems with an astounding variety of marine life that can be enjoyed with just a snorkel and fins. There are many, many excellent scuba and snorkeling sites off both the north and south shores, so if the wind is up on one side, you can simply head for the other.

Upon arrival at the airport you'll be greeted by a crowd of baggage handlers and taxi drivers vying for your business. The bigger resorts send drivers to meet guests at the plane; everyone else has to fend for themselves. The towns of Coxen Hole and French Harbour are close to the airport (Coxen Hole is about a ten-minute walk). Coxen Hole, named for pirate John Coxen, is a lively port and fishing town and the Bay Islands' capital. You'll find such staples as banks and pharmacies; a small, colorful central plaza; and a variety of general stores, plus a few gift shops selling crafts, T-shirts, and postcards. French Harbour is

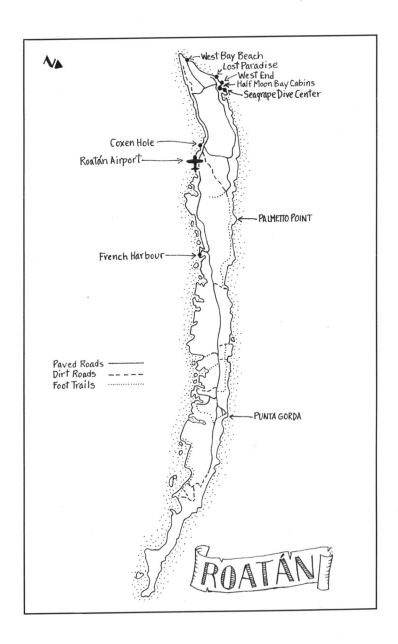

West Bay Beach
Lost Paradise
West End
Half Moon Bay Cabins
Seagrape Dive Center

Coxen Hole
Roatán Airport

PALMETTO POINT

French Harbour

Paved Roads ——————
Dirt Roads – – – –
Foot Trails ....

PUNTA GORDA

ROATÁN

Roatán's commercial center, with several shellfish packing plants and much shipping activity.

Most visitors, however, will end up in the little town of West End, which is a much longer cab ride (you shouldn't have to pay more than a few dollars per person, though the driver will try to charge more). *Collectivo* buses (minivans that say "Hilton" or "Taca Jr." on the side) or shared taxis are available from Coxen Hole to West End for less than $1 per person. West End, a shady enclave with one rutted dirt road serving as the main street, is a like miniature international village; take a short stroll and you'll hear conversations in German, Italian, English (of several varieties), and Spanish. Within a few days you'll know almost everyone, and newcomers are quickly shown the ropes by visitors who've been here a bit longer.

West End's main street runs parallel to the shore, with businesses on both sides, some built on stilts out over the water. Less than a mile long, the street bustles with activity from the early hours of the morning, when the first dive boats head out. Every other establishment seems to be a dive shop, and all are doing a brisk business. The dozens of little restaurants quickly fill up with those who aren't quite so ambitious early in the day. A constant stream of taxis, their horns honking, bump back and forth over the rutted road. Parrots squawk from cages and roosters crow and strut in the yards. The crowds thin during the day as people head out to enjoy Roatán's sights and activities, but in the evening, the restaurants and cabanas, their lights twinkling in the dusk, hum once again, as the sunburned adventurers swap stories over a cold beer.

Lost Paradise Resort, West End, Roatán

But West End has much more to offer than a bite to eat, a place to lay your head, and the opportunity to participate in water sports. You can stock up on reading material or book a tour of the island at the Casi Todo Bookstore, whose owners have a wealth of information about Roatán. Signs posted in stores and restaurants advertise horseback riding, glass-bottom boat tours, barbecues, and dances, among other things. A few shops sell T-shirts, postcards, maps, and a small selection of crafts; the Coco Plum Gift Shop also has a handy free map of West End that lists businesses, including prices and phone numbers. There's a soccer field just outside town, and the kids staying at Jimmy's have a perpetual volleyball game going. In the evenings the Bamboo Hut restaurant shows movies for $1. What you won't find in West End is much of a nightlife scene—no discos or bars (French Harbour has some), just restaurants that serve liquor, and those close at 11 p.m. This is an early-rising town.

For those who want to venture to the rest of the island, *collectivo* buses provide cheap and easy transportation to Coxen Hole and points beyond. The road to the east end was paved a few years ago, making the communities of Oak Ridge, Jonesville, and Punta Gorda more accessible, but also opening the area up for development, which is already moving ahead rapidly. Still, the eastern part of Roatán is remote and relatively undeveloped, providing a pleasant change of pace.

Further to the east are the little islands of Helene, Morat, and Barbareta. On Barbareta, a privately owned nature preserve, you'll find many of the plants and animals that have all but disappeared from Roatán, including wild

Photo by Eileen Ecklund

Church in West End, Roatán

parrots. Day trips to Barbareta are available through Casi Todo Bookstore in West End; you can choose a gentle nature walk that includes snorkeling and lunch at the beach lodge, or a more strenuous five-hour hike that includes a visit to a Payan archeological site. The cost is $35 per person; unfortunately that does not include transportation to the island, which is quite expensive ($50 round trip per person by boat, and almost $100 by plane). It's also possible to stay overnight at the lodge or in a bungalow, which, because of the high cost of transportation, may be the best option for those who want to visit Barbareta.

NOTEWORTHY

If conditions are favorable, snorkeling from West Bay beach, with its extensive reefs just offshore, is a delight, and the wide swath of pristine beach is a pleasant place to spend the afternoon sunning and swimming. The reefs in Half Moon Bay, also easily reached from shore, offer a very different but equally rich variety of marine life.

The Roatán Museum and the Institute for Marine Sciences, both located within Anthony's Key Resort, are well worth a visit. The museum has a small but interesting collection of artifacts illustrating different periods of Roatán's history, with excellent explanatory text in English and Spanish. Here you'll get a good sense of the mix (and occasional clash) of peoples that have made the Bay Islands the cultural polyglot it is today. The Institute for Marine Sciences' exhibit is devoted to the islands' natural resources, with displays on wildlife, geology, vegetation, and, of course, the reefs. Both the IMS and the Bay Islands

Conservation Association (BICA) are committed to conservation and environmental education on the islands. Admission to both these exhibits is $4 per person (sometimes the *Coconut Telegraph*, the Bay Islands magazine, has a free coupon insert); this price also gains you admission to the resort's dolphin show.

The privately owned Carambola Botanical Gardens, directly across the road from the entrance to Anthony's Key Resort, showcases both native and exotic plants, including orchids, spices, fruit trees, and native medicinals. There is also a trail that leads to the top of Mount Carambola, a not-too-steep hike of about 20 minutes, with excellent views from the summit. The "Iguana Wall," a historic breeding ground for iguanas and parrots, is a disappointment—you can't see any iguanas, and the wild parrots have pretty much disappeared from Roatán—but you may spot some lizards in the garden itself. General admission is $3 per person, but for an additional $2, you can take a guided tour and learn about the plants and their uses in greater detail.

One of the best ways to see the more remote portions of the island is to take the half-day tour offered by the owners of Casi Todo Books and Tours in West End ($25 per person). You'll visit Punta Gorda, the main settlement of the Garifuna people on the eastern end of the island, and Marble Hill Farms, where jellies are made using native hibiscus, mango, and other fruits. You'll also take a water taxi from Oak Ridge town through canals carved through the mangroves, where you can spot crabs among the tangled roots, and herons and egrets wading through the shallows. Views from the main road running along the island's ridge are spectacular. It's also possible to take a bus (very cheap) or taxi (very expensive) to other parts of the island, or rent a car for $48 a day, but you'll learn much more from the informative and friendly tour guide. Another option is to take a boat tour from Oak Ridge to Port Royal, where there are remnants of forts built by the British in the 18th century.

For a beautiful hike from West End, take the big dirt road that splits off from the main highway just outside the village, and head toward West Bay beach. The road climbs the ridge behind West End village, providing spectacular views of ocean and island—particularly near sunset—and a chance to get a closer look at the island's lush vegetation. Only the most avid hikers will want to go all the way out to the beach, a strenuous up-and-down haul of several miles, but there are excellent viewpoints within a half-hour's walk from town.

WHERE TO STAY

Roatán offers the widest range of accommodations in the Bay Islands, from a bare-bones room in Coxen Hole at $8/double, to the luxurious all-inclusive dive resorts costing hundreds of dollars per night. If you're a serious diver, the resorts can be a good deal—in fact, they offer some of the best package dive deals in the Caribbean. Among those highly recommended are Anthony's Key Resort, Fantasy Island, and the CocoView Resort. One of the best sources for information on these and other Honduras resort destinations is Roatán Charter, Box 877, San Antonio, FL 33576-0877, U.S. telephone: (800) 282-8932 or (904) 588-4132;

fax: (904) 588-4158. For the best all-around experience of the island, however, we recommend staying in one of the small but comfortable establishments in West End village.

Lost Paradise Resort
West End
Roatán, Bay Islands, Honduras
Telephone: (011) 504-45-1306; fax: (011) 504-45-1388
Situated at the south end of West End village where the town's main dirt road starts to peter out, Lost Paradise is a bit removed from the hustle and bustle, yet close enough to the town center for convenience. This is a friendly, casual, family-run place. Very pleasant wood cabins are built on the resort's private beach, which also features a cabana built over the water. The cabins, which sleep three comfortably, are $50 for those with ceiling fans, $62 with air conditioning. All have showers with hot running water. Rooms are also available in the resort's small motel for $12 per single, $20 per double, but this is an older building and not nearly as nice as the cabins.

Half Moon Bay Cabins
West End
Roatán, Bay Islands, Honduras
Telephone/fax: (011) 504-45-1075
This little resort of 14 cabins is even more secluded than the Lost Paradise, but its popular restaurant and bar provide their own center of activity, and the main part of town is still only a five-minute walk. Perched on the rough coral shelf that is the northern curve of Half Moon Bay, just to the north of West End village, the Half Moon Bay Cabins

offer excellent snorkeling right outside your front door. The accommodations are very similar to those at Lost Paradise—simply furnished but nice wood cabins, showers with hot running water—with a few extras, such as complimentary use of kayaks and snorkeling equipment, and pitchers of purified ice water in the rooms. Rates run $30 for a single, $45 for double rooms with ceiling fans; $45 per single and $60 per double for air conditioning. Triple and quad rates range from $55 to $90. The management here is also very helpful and friendly, and the exchange rate offered is one of West End's best.

RESTAURANTS

The food on the Bay Islands is unlikely to be the high point of anyone's visit, although it's reputed to be quite decent (and relatively expensive) at the resorts. Fried fish, fried chicken, hamburgers, and french fries are staples, and the oil used for frying isn't always the best quality. For the most part, it's best to avoid chicken and beef. However, Roatán boasts a few restaurants that are excellent by any standards. One of the best is West End's Bite on the Beach, fondly known around town as "The Bite." Although set back a bit from the water, the Bite is indeed on the beach, a few minutes' walk from where the road ends on the south side of the village. Rustic picnic tables set amidst the trees take on a romantic glow when the kerosene lanterns are lit at nightfall. Here you can enjoy wonderfully spiced and carefully prepared fish and seafood dishes served with rice and vegetables, as well as such specialties as roast pork with pickled onions. Entrees average about $4 to $5 per person.

Another good choice is Mr. Foster's restaurant at West Bay Beach, reachable by water taxi. (Foster's restaurant right in town is passable but not as good.) The Dutch chef makes a terrific appetizer of calamari with corn and tomato salsa, and if you catch a fish, they'll cook it for you. Prices are in the same range as The Bite's.

For simpler and less expensive island food, try Stanley's, up a path and a short flight of stairs off of West End's main road (look for the sign just north of the Sunset Inn). The tasty fish and seafood dishes, such as shrimp sauteed with garlic, onions, and peppers, are complemented by spicy rice and beans and a huge basket of homemade coconut bread, all for about $3 or $4. Another place specializing in island food is Island Breeze, near the Half Moon Bay Cabins; be sure to visit when conch stew is on the menu.

Should you develop a craving for pasta, hike down the beach past The Bite for about five minutes, just past the first plank bridge skirting the rocks, to Keifitos' Plantation Resort. The restaurant is perched on a deck up in the trees, overlooking the water—a great place to catch the sunset (be sure to bring a flashlight for the walk back, though). Run by an Italian family, Keifitos' restaurant serves an array of good seafood pasta and other entrees, including a good sauteed conch. Prices average about $5 to $6. Rooms and cabins are also available.

For a splurge, take a cab to French Harbour and dine at Gio's. One of the islands' fanciest restaurants, Gio's is also relatively expensive—which means that the restaurant's specialty, a king crab bigger than your head, is about $13. Other items on the menu, from fish and seafood to steaks and pasta, are a good bit cheaper. The atmosphere is casual, the service friendly, and the view out over the water is lovely at night.

For breakfasts, the Bamboo Hut and the Coffee Stop both serve pancakes, eggs, and various other staples, at very good prices. The Bamboo Hut also offers fresh baked goods (try the banana bread if it's available), wonderful cinnamon-spiked coffee, and *baleadas*, an island specialty of beans, cheese, and various other ingredients wrapped in a tortilla.

FROM MY JOURNAL

Today we snorkeled off West Bay beach, where the reefs are just a few kicks of the flipper from shore. Both beach and water were relatively crowded, but out there is an entirely different universe. We rarely saw another snorkeler as we wended our way through and outside the huge system of reefs, to the point where the ocean floor dropped away beneath us. The water was pristine and so clear that it seemed you could see forever. We hung suspended over the drop-off, awestruck by the immensity of this under-water world.

Closer in we were greeted by a riot of color and activity: triggerfish, angelfish, huge green and purple parrotfish, rock beauties, sergeant majors, redfin needlefish, squirrelfish, and the occasional barracuda. Purple sea fans waved lazily from coral outcrops, flounders burrowed into the sand far below. Back on shore we discovered that we'd been out for hours and had managed, despite gobs of sunscreen, to get a good burn on our backs. It's easy to lose track of time out there.

In the evening we ate a wonderful dinner at the West Bay beach restaurant, then took the water taxi back to the village. During the day the taxis are boisterous, crowded with sunbathers and snorkelers headed out for a day's fun. Tonight the few passengers were subdued, quietly enjoying the ride as the boat skimmed through the dark, sparks of phosphor shooting through the wake. We ran without lights, the pilot occasionally slowing to shine a flashlight and get his bearings.

Back now at our hotel, we sit on the veranda sipping a beer and listening to the soft strains of reggae music coming from a cabana perched out over the water. A tiny hummingbird nesting on the porch is settling in for the night and, worn out from a long day of sun, surf, and snorkeling, we decide to do the same.

HOW TO GET THERE

From the United States, Taca Airlines (800-535-8780) has weekly nonstop flights to Roatán from Miami, New Orleans, and Houston; weekday flights from Miami to Roatán stop in San Pedro Sula, on the mainland. Taca also has occasional flights from Los Angeles to Roatán that stop in San Salvador and San Pedro Sula. If you're starting from mainland Honduras, you can fly to Roatán from Tegucigalpa, San Pedro Sula, and La Ceiba. Both Sosa and Isleña have several daily flights from La Ceiba for about $10, or you can take the ferry for less.

Guanaja

Just a short flight away from Roatán, Guanaja seems as if it could easily be on another planet. While mobs of cab drivers will greet you at the Roatán airport, here you'll find a few small boys vying to carry your bags. Where Roatán has almost finished a sparkling new international terminal, on Guanaja, a few thatch-roofed huts next to the airstrip provide refreshment and a shady waiting area. From the roof of one hut someone with a sense of humor has hung a Salva Vida beer sign that says "Concourse B." There is only one road on Guanaja and one car, which doesn't work. People get around by motorbike, bike, horse, foot, and, of course, boat. Your first activity on Guanaja will be to take a water taxi from the airport into town.

Guanaja is a green, hilly, relatively uninhabited island of about 29 square miles. It was dubbed the "Isle of Pines" by Christopher Columbus, because of the Caribbean pine forests covering its steep slopes. Unfortunately, many of those slopes have been deforested, with thick pine stands remaining on only the most inaccessible. Still, Guanaja seems untouched in comparison to Roatán; most of its population is settled just offshore in the town of Bonacca on Hog Cay.

Bonacca is a colorful place, with houses on stilts lining the canals and waterways that crisscross the cay. The cay itself has been expanded with fill to about 17 acres, upon which some 5,000 people now live. As we made our way through the narrow, twisting, crowded streets, we found our eyes drawn to the uninhabited peaks rising from the nearby main island and wondering why Bonaccans choose to cram themselves into this little space—but that was before we became acquainted with the main island's sandfly population. There are a few people who have braved the sandflies, however, and established small settle-

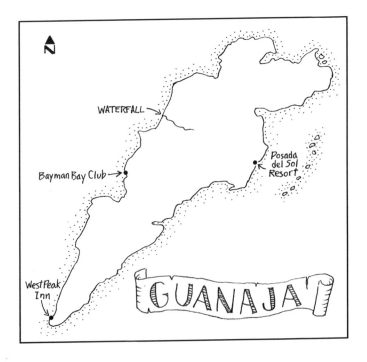

Savannah Bight, Guanaja

ments at Savannah Bight, Mangrove Bight, and North East Bight on Guanaja itself. Houses also dot the smaller cays.

On our first night on Hog Cay, in a hotel room just a few feet from the water's edge, the wind came off the ocean in a fury, battering at doors and carrying off anything not firmly nailed down. It blew so fiercely that the trees fringing the shore bent over nearly horizontal, and we thought the waves might reach our porch. We wondered if there were a storm brewing, but apparently high winds are common, providing blessed relief from heat and insects. I'd hate to be there for a really big blow: the last big hurricane, 1974's *Fifi*, took many of Bonacca's frail stilt houses with it. Some say that a few ended up on Roatán, where they were hauled up on land and put to use.

Bonaccans are very friendly and willing to accommodate visitors. Much more Spanish is spoken than on the other Bay Islands, but you'll have no problem getting around with just English. Fishing is the main industry, with tourism on the rise. Most visitors head for one of the excellent dive-oriented resorts, such as the Bayman Bay Club and Posada del Sol, which are pricy but offer a wide variety of activities and amenities. For more information about Guanaja's resorts, contact Roatán Charter, P.O. Box 877, San Antonio, FL 33576-0877; U.S. telephone: (800) 282-8932 or (904) 588-4132; fax: (904) 588-4158.

Even if you're not staying at one of the resorts, you'll find plenty to do and see on Guanaja, including snorkeling, beaching, diving, fishing, and hiking. Arrangements for a boat can easily be made in Bonacca, and prices are reasonable (and usually negotiable). We found our guide, Feliciano, by way of his sidekick Eric, a small boy who hangs around the Hotel Alexander and seems to know everyone.

Change is coming to Guanaja. Small cabins are springing up here and there around the main island, and more yachters are discovering the delights of the offshore cays. But the pace of change is slow, and it's still easy to find a solitude that is all too rare on Roatán. For now at least, visitors will find this island a relaxing sojourn from the outside world.

NOTEWORTHY

Bonacca town, dubbed the "Venice of Honduras," may not have the architecture or sights of its Italian cousin, but it's a fascinating, frenetic maze of streets and canals. Bonacca is a hive of activity (except during the afternoon siesta, when everything shuts down for a few hours), with people scurrying about, hard at work or socializing in the many little restaurants and stores. Although the town is fairly small, it's easy to spend a morning or evening getting lost here just wandering around and absorbing the atmosphere. Don't expect much in the way of nightlife, though; there's even less here than on Roatán.

The only way to see the rest of Guanaja is to hire a boat in Bonacca to ferry you around. You can arrange a trip to one of the multitude of little cays for an afternoon of swimming, snorkeling, and sun, or head through the canal to the other side of the island, where you can see the monument at Christopher Columbus' landing site or take a short hike to a waterfall. Arrangements can also be made in town to dive, snorkel, or fish. There are numerous trails to explore on the main island, with or without a guide. The steep slopes provide wonderful views and the opportunity to stumble across Indian artifacts.

Even if you don't plan to stay there, take a boat ride around to the West Peak Inn. There you can have three miles of palm-lined beach practically to yourself, swim, snorkel, and enjoy a meal or cold drink in the open-air cabana. David Greatorex, a former British marine engineer who has "retired" to build and run the West Peak, and his right-hand man, Ashbert, are friendly and attentive hosts, with many stories to tell and plenty of information about Guanaja.

WHERE TO STAY

Hotel Alexander

Bonacca

Guanaja, Bay Islands, Honduras

Telephone: (011) 504-45-4326

Outside of the resorts, this is the best hotel on Guanaja, but it's not exactly luxurious. The rooms are simple and clean, with ceiling fans or air conditioning, and the showers have hot running water (usually). The Alexander's main advantage is that it's situated out at the end of the cay, right at water's edge, where it gets the benefit of the ocean breezes; hotels in town can be claustrophobic and stuffy. Ask for a room on the sea side, and you'll get your own covered porch with lounge chairs looking out over the water. Rates are $17 for a double.

Photo by Randy Zebell

West Peak Inn, Guanaja

Hotel Miller
Bonacca
Guanaja, Bay Islands, Honduras
Telephone: (011) 504-45-4327
Offers clean, very basic rooms with ceiling fan or air conditioning for $10-$20 per double. There is also a small dining room serving decent food.

West Peak Inn
Guanaja, Bay Islands, Honduras
Fax: (011) 504-45-4219
Owner David Greatorex is just getting this remote and still rather rustic establishment off the ground. When we visited he had completed an open air restaurant/bar just back from the beach, with a bathroom and shower building next to it and four tent cabins situated in the trees behind. By the end of 1995 he plans to have transformed the tent cabins into four "luxury" cabins with their own bathrooms, showers, and electric lights. The food is some of the best on Guanaja, and the atmosphere is friendly and relaxed; guests help themselves to drinks when Greatorex isn't around, marking their tally down in a book he keeps on the bar. If the generator holds out, you can watch one of the videos Greatorex's family and friends send down to him. Rates are $25 per person, which includes meals. To get to West Peak, ask a water taxi to take you to "Mr. David's," and be sure to bring a flashlight and plenty of insect repellent or baby oil for the sandflies.

RESTAURANTS

If you stay at one of the resorts, it's unlikely that you'll want to eat anywhere else. There are little restaurants sprinkled throughout Bonacca town, very few of them with signs out front or even formal names. The best you can say about the food is that it's uniformly unremarkable. We had the best luck with local specialties such as stewed chicken and rice and beans. For breakfast or lunch, try Restaurant TKO just down the street from Hotel Alexander—prices are very cheap and the food is reasonable. Other possibilities include Joe's and the Hotel Miller's dining room.

By far the best food outside of the resorts (and, proprietor David Greatorex claims, even better than the food *in* the resorts) is to be found at the West Peak Inn, a new establishment on the island's west side. Although it's not fully set up as a restaurant yet, "Mr. David's" has served tasty meals to many of Guanaja's visitors—and to quite a few of the locals, as well. When you eat here you'll get what's available for that day (there's no menu), but you won't have cause for complaint. One night we had an excellent coconut curried chicken adapted from an East African recipe; another time we had wonderfully tasty smoked pork chops with mashed potatoes. If you're staying at the West Peak, all meals are included; otherwise you'll end up paying less than $10 per person.

FROM MY JOURNAL

Sitting out on the pier at the West Peak Inn at night, we're surrounded by sea and stars and the soft, warm breeze. The quiet would be immense if it weren't for the water lapping at the pier and the faint hum of the Inn's generator, which tonight is powering the video player, so our fellow guests can watch a movie. It's hard to believe that just this morning we were in hectic Bonacca town, with its maze of narrow, winding streets and constant rush of humanity.

We're sunburnt and a bit weary from a long day of boating around the island to see the sights. But what sights they were: the mountainous, pine-forested mass of Guanaja's interior rising steeply from its palm-fringed beaches; the brilliant turquoise sea dotted with dozens of sandy cays; two dolphins cresting the waves as they escorted our boat; an islander snorkeling out far from shore in search of lobster, towing his canoe behind him. And finally, a hike through lush forest and up a rocky stream bed to see a waterfall splashing down from the slopes above.

For a while we beam the flashlight down beneath the pier, watching the schools of silvery little fish mass and swirl in the water below. When we turn it off and turn our heads skyward, the sheer number of stars is breathtaking. Soon little points of phosphorescence begin to wink underwater, mirroring the fireflies above. West Peak's proprietor has told us that sometimes when he swims at night, the phosphor is so thick it seems his whole body is glowing.

A few days later, as we boat around to catch our plane, the island's peaks are shrouded in cloud and mist, the dark sky promising a rain it soon delivers. We don't mind getting a bit soggy; it's worth it to see this other face of Guanaja, as beautiful in its own way as the sparkling, sunlit island we saw yesterday.

Photo by Randy Zebell

The airport at Guanaja

HOW TO GET THERE

From Roatán, Sosa airlines has one direct flight daily (except Sundays) to Guanaja, departing at 10 a.m. Both Sosa and Isleña have daily (except Sundays) flights from La Ceiba, on the mainland. From either, the cost is about $10 one-way, although a price increase was expected when we visited.

Utila

Utila is the smallest and least populated of the three main Bay Islands, and usually gets short shrift in the few travel guides that mention it. It's true that there isn't a huge variety of things to do, and the accommodations and food are far from deluxe. But if you're an avid diver or snorkeler, or just someone looking for a very relaxed atmosphere and low prices, Utila can be a good bet indeed.

At first we weren't even sure we'd be able to get to the island. Stuck in a torrential downpour in La Ceiba, on the mainland, we learned that Utila's airstrip had been forced to shut down. Fortunately, the next morning the skies had cleared, but as we climbed aboard the rickety nine-seater plane, one of our fellow passengers told us that she was back for a second try at flying over: the plane had refused to start earlier that morning.

This bit of news had us all chuckling nervously as one of the engines balked, then finally sputtered into life. As we taxied down the runway, the pilot peering out of his opened side window, we wondered what we were getting into. But the short flight to the island was fine, and

Photo by Randy Zebell

A typical East Harbour home

we bumped down on to the tiny dirt runway without incident.

Utila has a character and charm that is distinctly different from either Roatán or Guanaja. Its main settlement, the tidy little town of East Harbour, is dominated by cheery wood cottages decorated with scalloped roof and porch trim. Many of the brightly painted little homes peek out from a lush covering of bougainvillea and other tropical foliage. The British influence is strong here; many of the inhabitants are descendants of British settlers from the Cayman Islands. Most speak an island English that has a very musical lilt, even when they're good-naturedly trading jibes, as they frequently do. Utilans are generally very friendly, and visitors are made to feel welcome.

With only some 2,000 inhabitants, East Harbour is a

small but lively place. That is in large part due to the presence of crowds of young, impoverished adventurers who find their way here for the cheapest scuba diving in the Caribbean (PADI certification starts at about $125, with free lodging often thrown in). Those who aren't out diving are strolling the town's main street or gathering in one of its restaurants or bars to drink, talk, and write letters home.

The island of Utila is some 16 square miles in size, much of it taken up by an interior mangrove swamp. It's quite flat—the highest point, Pumpkin Hill, is about 200 feet—and ringed by the barrier reef that is its main attraction. There are almost no beaches on Utila itself. A few small cays lie offshore.

Diving is definitely the main attraction here, and opportunities are plentiful and cheap. Other water sports, such as snorkeling, fishing, and even waterskiing, can be easily arranged through one of several establishments along East Harbour's main street. Although it's possible to snorkel and swim just offshore from the airport, the best sites are reputed to be around the nearby cays.

Exploring Utila on foot doesn't take too much time; the main attractions are a stroll around East Harbour and out to Sandy Bay, and a three-mile hike out to Pumpkin Hill beach. Bikes are also available for rent. There are more possibilities if you hire a boat to take you exploring: waterways through the mangroves, the offshore cays, and Turtle Harbour Marine Reserve (which is said to have spectacular undersea canyons) on the other side of the island. Depending on where you go, prices can range from a few dollars per person, to $20 or more.

Utila is also a good jumping-off spot for Cayos

Cochinos (Hog Cays), part of the Bay Islands chain. These little cays have few tourist developments and are largely uninhabited, except for some Garifuna fishing settlements. You can make arrangements for a day trip to or stay on one of the Cayos Cochinos through the Green House Tours and Book Exchange in East Harbour.

NOTEWORTHY

East Harbour is well worth an afternoon of leisurely exploring, to soak up the atmosphere and admire the colorful cottages. Be sure to stop by the office of the Bay Islands Conservation Association on the main street, which has a small exhibit on Utila's marine life, as well as both conservation and tourist information. This is a good place to buy a colorful T-shirt supporting BICA. Gunther's Gallerie (follow the signs from the main street) has nice hand-drawn maps of Utila and other souvenir items for sale.

Orma's Restaurant, a breezy little thatch-roofed place built out over the water, is a good spot to relax and with a beer and chat with other visitors. You can also play checkers or backgammon on "boards" carved into the picnic tables; old bottle caps serve as the game pieces. The most notable watering hole, however, is the Bucket of Blood, popular with visitors and locals alike and a good source for information on the island and its history.

Hiking or boating to Pumpkin Hill, with its small beach and nearby caves to explore, is also recommended.

WHERE TO STAY

Just about every other place in East Harbour and its extension, Sandy Bay, seems to be offering rooms for rent, whether they're in a private home or a "hotel" (they're more like rooming houses, really). They're all pretty much the same, too: very bare-bones but clean, with a ceiling fan and shared or private bath, sometimes with hot water. Most are also $10 or less for two people; some offer reduced rates or free rooms if you're taking a PADI scuba certification course through their diving center.

Trudy's

East Harbour
Utila, Bay Islands, Honduras
Telephone: (011) 504-45-3195
Trudy's is one of Utila's best-known hotels, just a short walk from the airport. It's clean, friendly, cheap, and very basic, although the owners were in the process of renovating the rooms (some to include air conditioning) while we were there. Breakfast is available in a dining room downstairs, and there's a dive center attached. Rates are $10 for a double.

Harbour View Hotel

East Harbour
Utila, Bay Islands, Honduras
Rooms here are a bit bigger than at Trudy's, and there's a pleasant deck with tables and chairs. The Parrot Dive Centre is attached. Rates are $10 per double.

Utila Lodge Resort

East Harbour
Utila, Bay Islands, Honduras
Telephone: (011) 504-45-3143; fax: (011) 504-45-3209
The one exception to the standard accommodations on Utila is this dive resort, which offers fancier rooms with private baths, hot water, and air conditioning. Built right out over the water, the Utila Lodge also has a lounge and restaurant, gift shop and, of course, diving facilities. Rates are $50 per double; if you want to eat in the restaurant, it's an extra $50 per couple for three meals a day. Dive packages are also available.

RESTAURANTS

There are scads of restaurants in East Harbour, many of them run right out of people's homes, but we were unable to find one that had food any better than merely passable. Many offer fish, seafood, and local specialties on the menu, but few actually had any when we visited. Thompson's Bakery is an exception, and reputed to be (it was closed when we visited) one of the best in Utila, offering such island specialties as conch soup and curried chicken. Prices are very cheap, averaging only a few dollars per person. Thompson's also serves substantial breakfasts and sells baked goods. Look for it just off East Harbour's main street, on the way to the Bucket of Blood bar.

The Tropical Sunset, one of the biggest and fanciest restaurants, has a huge menu, very little of which was available. An edible cheeseburger and fries here will set you back about $2; other items might go as high as $5. The

Tropical Sunset is just a few doors up from Thompson's.

Other choices include Selly's, for "international and creole cuisine" (actually, the main attraction here seems to be the TV), the Manhattan, Mary's, the Seven Seas, and the Mermaid. Expect to pay only a few dollars per person.

You can also eat at the Utila Lodge, but if you aren't a guest, you must make arrangements in advance. Expect prices to be substantially higher.

FROM MY JOURNAL

Despite its tiny size, East Harbour was awhirl with activity when we arrived, and not just because of all the tourists. The locals seem to be in constant motion, adults zipping along the main street in little motorized carts or on scooters, kids doing the same on bicycles. There are also a few pickup trucks—one serves as the island's only taxi, ferrying passengers from the airport into town—a fair-sized complement of vehicles for a town that only has one short road and a few side streets.

At the port men were busy loading and unloading ships, trundling handcarts filled with boxes, furniture, and huge bags of rice. Construction crews hammered away, renovating houses and hotels. Old men sat in front of the shops, swapping stories and calling out to passersby. Rock music blasted from a rooming house.

At midday most of the activity came grinding to a halt for siesta, the heat of the day driving people indoors. But today was different from most days—one of the townspeople had died, and businesses were closed all afternoon. People dressed in their best clothes gathered in groups to walk to the bereaved family's house, many of the women carrying flowers or dishes of food. This is a tiny, close-knit town, and most of the villagers attended the funeral; in fact, people had been coming in all day from the mainland and the other islands.

Now that it's evening and respects have been paid, the activity has resumed. Kids once again wheel their bikes down the main street, shouting and laughing. Voices sing out from the church, where evening service is being conducted. Locals and visitors alike gather in open air restaurants and bars to enjoy a beer and the cooling night breezes. But everyone rises early in the morning to go to work or head out on the dive boats; soon groups of people begin to wind their way home, and quiet falls over East Harbour.

Photo by Randy Zebell

Carved wooden balconies, East Harbour, Utila

HOW TO GET THERE

From Roatán, Sosa has two flights daily (except Sunday) to Utila with a stopover in La Ceiba. Both Sosa and Islena have several flights daily (except Sunday) between La Ceiba and Utila. It costs about $10 to fly between any one of the islands and La Ceiba, although a price increase was expected when we visited. There is also a ferry that runs once daily between Utila, La Ceiba, and Roatán; at about $10 for the whole trip, it is cheaper than flying, but takes almost a whole day. You can also hire a boat on Roatán to take you to Utila, but it will cost much more than flying.

PRACTICAL TIPS

Immigration: For U.S. citizens, only a passport is currently required to visit Honduras. All foreigners visiting the Bay Islands must pay an entry and exit tax at the airport; at the time of this writing, they were $2 and $10, respectively. Be sure to reconfirm any airline reservations you have, both within Honduras and for your return home, several days before departure.

Flights: It is quite easy to fly directly to Roatán from the United States or from Tegucigalpa, San Pedro Sula, and La Ceiba on mainland Honduras. Flying to the islands of Utila or Guanaja from the United States, however, will require an overnight stopover either on the mainland or on Roatán.

Direct flights are offered from Roatán to either Utila or Guanaja , but not from these islands back to Roatán. To fly from Utila or Guanaja to Roatan, or to fly between Utila and Guanaja, you must go through La Ceiba. The island-hopper flights are inexpensive, but you may get stuck in La Ceiba overnight if you miss a connection, or if the plane is full.

Information and arrangements: Roatán Charter (904-588-4132 or toll-free at 800-282-8932 in the U.S.) is an excellent and very friendly source of information about the Bay Islands and mainland Honduras, and can make arrangements for stays at any of the major resorts or on live-aboard dive boats.

Currency: At the time we visited, the exchange rate for Honduran currency, the lempira (or lemp, as everyone calls it), was about nine per U.S. dollar. If you stay at one of the all-inclusive dive resorts on any of the three islands, you may never need to change money, since they tend to prefer U.S. dollars or credit cards. In fact, many establishments on Roatán, and particularly in West End, do accept dollars, but usually won't give you a very good exchange rate. The best exchange rates are offered by the banks and at some of the hotels. Traveler's checks are easy to cash (most of the hotels will do it), but only the biggest establishments will be able to handle large denominations. Quite a few hotels on Roatán accept credit cards, but most charge about ten percent extra if you choose to pay this way.

Prices: The Bay Islands are substantially more expensive than mainland Honduras because virtually everything, from food, to building materials, to purified water, has to be shipped in. Still, most North Americans and Europeans will find prices here a bargain, especially compared to those in other Caribbean destinations. Prices do tend to change rapidly and without warning, however; the cost to fly between islands went up 40 percent overnight while we were there.

Health: There is cholera in Honduras, so take the normal precautions regarding food and don't drink unpurified water or ice. Malaria medication is also recommended. Probably the biggest health concern for visitors, however, is the sun, which can be brutal. Bring plenty of sunblock, a broad-brimmed hat, and light, long-sleeved shirts and pants, and remember to drink lots of water. The Bay Islands' sandflies are legendary, and deservedly so—in a few moments they can cover you with bites that will itch for a week. Avon's Skin So Soft is reputed to work well against them, but we used plain old baby oil—they stick to it and expire before they can sting. Insect repellent with DEET also works.

Language: Both English and Spanish are spoken. English is still the most prevalent, but Spanish is common (particularly on Guanaja and in some parts of Roatán), and many mainlanders who have moved to the islands speak no English.

Be sure to pick up a copy of the *Coconut Telegraph* during your stay. This little English language magazine is packed full of interesting articles and information about the islands and their inhabitants, and only costs about $1. Finally, it's a good idea to bring a flashlight for walking around at night.

Epilogue

Island enthusiasts, take note: there are many more undiscovered islands not included in this book. This was especially true in the seemingly endless chain of Family Islands in the Bahamas. Beyond Exuma and Long Island lie such hideaways as Farmer's Cay, Crooked Island, Acklins, the Jumento Cays (Ragged Island, Flamingo Cay, Nurse Cay), and Mayaguana Island.

Enchanted islands sometimes appear where you least expect them. During several visits to Marie-Galante and Les Saintes in the French West Indies, we bypassed an island that guidebooks described as "flat, barren, and uninhabited." But when we later ventured forth on our own, we were surprised to find a little jewel off Guadeloupe: an ancient south Atlantic mountain rising from the sea. An enchanting 18th-century village, wonderful beaches, and fine French cuisine awaited us as we stepped off the local ferry.

The Caribbean harbors many more such opportunities for discovery and exploration for the intrepid traveler willing to make the extra effort. The more challenging the journey, the greater the rewards of secluded destinations with undiscovered charms and hidden beauty.

I am always very happy to hear about your travels, and I'd like to hear from more of you. Please write to me directly at 2987 College Ave., Berkeley, CA 94705. Happy traveling!

Burl Willes

Index

Other Books from John Muir Publications

Travel Books by Rick Steves
Asia Through the Back Door, 4th ed., 400 pp. $17.95
Europe 101: History, Art, and Culture for the Traveler, 5th ed., 368 pp. $17.95
Mona Winks: Self-Guided Tours of Europe's Top Museums, 3rd ed., 432 pp. $18.95
Rick Steves' Best of the Baltics and Russia, 144 pp. $9.95
Rick Steves' Best of Europe, 544 pp. $16.95
Rick Steves' Best of France, Belgium, and the Netherlands, 240 pp. $12.95
Rick Steves' Best of Germany, Austria, and Switzerland, 240 pp. $12.95
Rick Steves' Best of Great Britain, 192 pp. $11.95
Rick Steves' Best of Italy, 208 pp. $11.95
Rick Steves' Best of Scandinavia, 192 pp. $11.95
Rick Steves' Best of Spain and Portugal, 192 pp. $11.95
Rick Steves' Europe Through the Back Door, 480 pp. $17.95
Rick Steves' French Phrase Book, 2nd ed., 176 pp. $4.95
Rick Steves' German Phrase Book, 2nd ed., 176 pp. $4.95
Rick Steves' Italian Phrase Book, 2nd ed., 176 pp. $4.95
Rick Steves' Spanish and Portuguese Phrase Book, 2nd ed., 304 pp. $5.95
Rick Steves' French/German/Italian Phrase Book, 320 pp. $6.95

A Natural Destination Series
Belize: A Natural Destination, 3rd ed., 336 pp. $16.95
Costa Rica: A Natural Destination, 3rd ed., 400 pp. $17.95
Guatemala: A Natural Destination, 2nd ed., 352 pp. $16.95

Undiscovered Islands Series
Undiscovered Islands of the Caribbean, 4th ed., 264 pp. $16.95
Undiscovered Islands of the Mediterranean, 2nd ed., 256 pp. $13.95
Undiscovered Islands of the U.S. and Canadian West Coast, 288 pp. $12.95

For Birding Enthusiasts
The Birder's Guide to Bed and Breakfasts: U.S. and Canada, 2nd ed., 416 pp. $17.95
The Visitor's Guide to the Birds of the Central National Parks: U.S. and Canada, 400 pp. $15.95
The Visitor's Guide to the Birds of the Eastern National Parks: U.S. and Canada, 400 pp. $15.95
The Visitor's Guide to the Birds of the Rocky Mountain National Parks: U.S. and Canada, 432 pp. $15.95

Unique Travel Series
Each is 112 pages and $10.95 paper, except Georgia.
Unique Arizona
Unique California
Unique Colorado
Unique Florida
Unique Georgia ($11.95)
Unique New England
Unique New Mexico
Unique Texas
Unique Washington

2 to 22 Days Itinerary Planners
2 to 22 Days in the American Southwest, 192 pp. $11.95
2 to 22 Days in Asia, 192 pp. $10.95
2 to 22 Days in Australia, 192 pp. $11.95
2 to 22 Days in California, 192 pp. $11.95
2 to 22 Days in Eastern Canada, 240 pp $12.95
2 to 22 Days in Florida, 192 pp. $11.95

2 to 22 Days Around the Great
Lakes, 192 pp. $11.95
2 to 22 Days in Hawaii, 192 pp.
$11.95
2 to 22 Days in New England, 192
pp. $11.95
2 to 22 Days in New Zealand, 192
pp. $11.95
2 to 22 Days in the Pacific
Northwest, 192 pp. $11.95
2 to 22 Days in the Rockies, 192
pp. $11.95
2 to 22 Days in Texas, 192 pp.
$11.95
2 to 22 Days in Thailand, 192 pp.
$10.95
22 Days Around the World, 264 pp.
$13.95

Other Terrific Travel Titles

The 100 Best Small Art Towns in
America, 224 pp. $12.95
The Big Book of Adventure Travel,
2nd ed., 384 pp. $17.95
Environmental Vacations:
Volunteer Projects to Save the
Planet, 2nd ed., 248 pp. $16.95
A Foreign Visitor's Guide to
America, 224 pp. $12.95
Great Cities of Eastern Europe,
256 pp. $16.95
Indian America: A Traveler's
Companion, 4th ed., 480 pp.
$18.95
Interior Furnishings Southwest,
256 pp. $19.95
Opera! The Guide to Western
Europe's Great Houses, 296 pp.
$18.95
The People's Guide to Mexico, 10th
ed., 608 pp. $19.95
Ranch Vacations: The Complete
Guide to Guest and Resort, Fly-
Fishing, and Cross-Country
Skiing Ranches, 3rd ed., 512 pp.
$19.95
The Shopper's Guide to Art and
Crafts in the Hawaiian Islands,
272 pp. $13.95
Understanding Europeans, 272 pp.
$14.95
Watch It Made in the U.S.A.:
A Visitor's Guide to the
Companies that Make Your
Favorite Products, 328 pp. $16.95

Parenting Titles

Being a Father: Family, Work, and
Self, 176 pp. $12.95
Teens: A Fresh Look, 240 pp. $14.95

Automotive Titles

The Greaseless Guide to Car Care,
2nd ed., 272 pp. $19.95
How to Keep Your Subaru Alive,
480 pp. $21.95
How to Keep Your Toyota Pickup
Alive, 392 pp. $21.95
How to Keep Your VW Alive, 25th
Anniversary ed., 472 pp. $25

Ordering Information

Please check your local bookstore for
our books, or call 1-800-888-7504 to
order direct. All orders are shipped
via UPS; see chart below to calculate
your shipping charge for U.S. destinations. No post office boxes
please; we must have a street
address to ensure delivery. If the
book you request is not available, we
will hold your check until we can ship
it. Foreign orders will be shipped surface rate unless otherwise requested;
please enclose $3 for the first item
and $1 for each additional item.

For U.S. Orders Totaling	Add
Up to $15.00	$4.25
$15.01 to $45.00	$5.25
$45.01 to $75.00	$6.25
$75.01 or more	$7.25

Methods of Payment

Check, money order, American
Express, MasterCard, or Visa. We
cannot be responsible for cash sent
through the mail. For credit card
orders, include your card number,
expiration date, and your signature,
or call 1-800-888-7504. American
Express card orders can only be
shipped to billing address of card-
holder. Sorry, no C.O.D.'s. Residents
of sunny New Mexico, add 6.25% tax
to total.

Address all orders and inquiries to:
John Muir Publications
P.O. Box 613
Santa Fe, NM 87504
(505) 982-4078
(800) 888-7504